World Championship

DUTCH OVEN

Cookbook

Credits

Photographers

Cover — Peter Christiansen

Logan Canyon

Northern Utah

Authors' Pictures — Caroline Patrick Jones

Copyright 1989

ISBN 0-9623918-0-8
First Printing June 1989
Second Printing January 1991
Third Printing April 1992
Fourth Printing September 1993
Fifth Printing May 1995
Sixth Printing March 1997
Seventh Printing May 1998
Eighth Printing May 1999
Ninth Printing May 2000
Tenth Printing December 2001
Eleventh Printing February 2003
Twelfth Printing July 2004
Thirteenth Printing January 2006
Fourteenth Printing January 2008
Fifteenth Printing February 2010
Sixteenth Printing February 2012

Printed by

watkins
P R I N T I N G
110 West 1200 South
Logan, Utah

World Championship
DUTCH OVEN
Cookbook

With recipes from the
World Championship Dutch Oven Cookoff

Juanita Kohler
Mike Kohler
Pat Kohler
Wallace Kohler
Pat Michaud
Dick Michaud

Illustrations by **Charles Yanito**

FOREWORD

It was Dian Thomas, television's outdoor cooking guru, who first told me about the wonderful food that "camp" cooks produce at the World Championship Dutch Oven Cookoff each year at the Festival of the American West in Logan, Utah. I was skeptical. I found it very hard to believe that Dutch oven cooks could, indeed, turn out lemon meringue pies and baked Alaskas that would delight a professional chef in a three-legged, black iron pot over a few hot coals. Her assurance that it was absolutely true, however, was sufficiently intriguing to make me want to see how they did it.

So I attended the Championship Cookoff as one of the judges and after watching — not camp cooks but everyday families, prepare their favorite recipes I was impressed. Then after sampling the 45 pots worth of beautiful breads, tender ribs and chicken, and tasty veggies and desserts that came out of those old, black ovens, I returned home a complete convert and realized that the historic Dutch oven of yesteryear was today's most versatile cooking system for family cooking anywhere in the out-of-doors.

Thus, when Dick and Pat Michaud and the Kohlers — Wallace and Pat, and Mike and Juanita, asked me to write the foreword to their new Dutch oven cookbook, I was delighted. For it was this group of Dutch oven experts who, as the committee behind the annual Cookoff, really made me a believer in this style of outdoor cooking.

I think the thing that impresses one most about the Dutch oven cookery is the ease with which even an amateur can follow the simple directions which experienced Dutch oven cooks like the Michauds and the Kohlers willingly provide. I also was impressed by how little space it takes to prepare a meal in one of the black pots. One can use them as easily on a postage stamp patio as in any small outdoor clearing. In this new book, the authors have provided not only the basics of Dutch oven cooking techniques, but a fund of other information, such as how to care for your pots and what kinds of equipment and accessories are handy to have. This cookbook is truly THE definitive primer on all levels of Dutch oven cooking. And the fact that the Michauds and the Kohlers have included numerous well-tested recipes from past Cookoffs as well as many of their own and those of their friends, is a genuine plus.

I highly recommend that you try the art of Dutch oven cooking for the fun and great tastes it will provide your family wherever you go for an activity — in the backyard, to the park, to a reunion, up the canyon or down a river. With a properly seasoned Dutch oven, a group of good friends or family, and this cookbook, you'll find you too are a convert to one of the oldest, yet simplest and most delicious, forms of outdoor cookery.

Betsy Balsley
Food Editor
LOS ANGELES TIMES

Acknowledgements

Many of the recipes in this cookbook are winning recipes from the Cookoffs of the past. Others have been gleaned from the experience of the authors. In all, they represent simple but delicious recipes to start with, intermediate ones to progress to, and finally, championship-winning recipes which will draw OOOHS and AAAHS from your family and friends. All of them will transmit to your tastebuds those doggone good tastes for which Dutch ovens are famous.

This cookbook is the result of the efforts of a number of people in addition to the authors. Special appreciation must go to all of the great folks who have been the contestants in the World Championship Dutch Oven Cookoff and who have produced many superior recipes contained herein. A thankful tip of the oven lid must go to Charles Yanito who took the ideas for illustrations and added his own interpretations and talent to make them all unique. Our family and friends have given much of their time and efforts in our support and we are very thankful to them. There have been many others who have contributed to our life's experience to bring us all to this point of publication and to all of them, we are grateful.

We have put together what we believe is a complete cookbook for all Dutch oven cooks. We hope that you enjoy every page and every recipe.

Introduction

Dutch ovens have been a part of America's history since colonial times. The big open fireplaces, whether in a fine home in Boston or a log cabin in Illinois, all had a place on the hearth for the uniquely-shaped black pots. The best sources indicate that the name "Dutch" oven came from the Dutch traders who went from door-to-door in colonies selling household wares. Paul Revere of revolutionary times and also a skilled metalsmith, is said to have fashioned the lid with its raised rim to hold the coals and the three stubby legs to give the oven more stability on the coals. Mary Washington, mother of our first president, thought so much of her "cast-iron kitchen furniture" that she addressed their disposal in her will.

The westward movement from the colonies saw many groups of people use the Dutch ovens in their travels. Lewis and Clark had one along when they explored the vast unknown of the northwest. Mountainmen made their stews and biscuits in the black pots while they were holed up in base camps waiting for the beaver pelts to reach their prime. Pioneers going to Oklahoma, Kansas, Utah, Oregon and California appreciated a layover for a day so that they could have some "lite" bread from the ovens. The famous chuckwagon on the cattle drives of the late 1800's had a special compartment in the "boot" for several Dutch ovens which were required to feed the bunch of hungry cowpunchers. Also sheepherders, miners, and lumbermen all relied on the ovens to cook the stews, steaks, biscuits and breads that maintained their health and good humor.

Today Dutch ovens are being used more than they ever were in days of old. They are becoming the country's favorite method of cooking outdoors. Not only do they cook meats, vegetables, breads and desserts, but the family can take them anywhere for fun and recreation. The backyard, the park, up the canyon, to the beach, at a church social, to camp, or down a river — all are suitable spots for the Dutch ovens to work their delicious art. Even inside the home, the black pots can be used in regular gas or electric ovens and still the recipes have that certain great taste that only Dutch ovens give to food.

To insure that the tradition of the black pot continues to grow and bless future generations, the World Championship Dutch Oven Cookoff, and its satellite cookoff system, has been founded. Hopefully, the Cookoff will serve as a catalyst for all dutchers and promote the fun and art of Dutch oven cooking for families everywhere. Its establishment as part of the nationally respected Festival of the American West in Logan, Utah, the state where more Dutch ovens are sold than any other, places it in the heartland of great Dutch oven cooking.

Table Of Contents

CHAPTER 8—

CHAPTER 9—

CHAPTER 10—

CHAPTER 1

How to Season, Care For and Use Your Dutch Oven

WHAT IS A DUTCH OVEN?

A camp Dutch oven is a cast iron pot varying in size from 8 to 22 inches in diameter. It has three legs about 1½ inches in length, a flat bottom and a lid that is flanged so it will hold hot coals or briquets. The lid has a low handle in the center and the Dutch oven has a bail on it similar to a bucket's bail. All of these features are for convenience in cooking over an open fire which is basically what the Dutch oven was designed to do.

In recent years, aluminum Dutch ovens have been manufactured and in addition to cooking over an open fire, both kinds can be adapted to cooking with briquets, on a Coleman stove, in your gas barbecue grill, or even in your kitchen with equal success. Dutch oven cooking in your kitchen oven would be more convenient if you used a Dutch oven without legs, rather than the camp Dutch oven.

The term "Camp Dutch Oven" is an old term and doesn't really reflect the versatility of this black pot. Dutch ovens are used not only while camping, but a great deal in back yards, on patios and in parks for family fun and for entertaining guests. Cooking outdoors is an easy way not to heat your house up on a warm summer day.

USES

A Dutch oven can be used in many different ways. You can literally cook anything in it. We have seen crepes, baked Alaska, candies and many other so called difficult dishes cooked to perfection. Breakfasts, main dishes, desserts, breads, side dishes — you name it, are easy to cook in your Dutch oven. Of course, a Dutch oven can be used to bake or roast anything that you would in a conventional oven. It is also self-basting. It can be used as a stew pot for cooking items you would normally cook on top of the kitchen range. It is a deep fryer, a steamer, and a frying pan. Turn the lid upside down and it is a grill. The Dutch oven is also a slow cooker or crock pot.

The weight of the lid helps to create a moisture seal while cooking and we are convinced that you also get a little pressure built up inside, making it work like a pressure cooker. If you want, you can stack two or three Dutch ovens on top of each other with coals in between and cook in this manner to maximize the use of your available coals.

A Dutch oven is generally made from heavy cast iron. Because of this, it heats evenly and holds its temperature longer. This keeps food being cooked from sticking and you don't have to use a lot of heat when cooking. A few coals go a long way.

When buying a Dutch oven for outdoor cooking be sure you don't get what we call a "bean pot"—one without legs and a flange on the lid. These two characteristics are very important and are used for controlling the temperature when cooking. The bail on the Dutch oven also has two positions. When folded down, it is much higher on one side of the oven than the other. When putting the oven in the fire, be sure it is in the up position. This is to prevent the bail from overheating and bending when you pick up a heavy, full Dutch oven. The down position of the bail is for storage.

Recently, many import Dutch ovens have come on the market. At first glance these ovens look good. However, in our experience, many of these ovens have thin spots in the casting, a rough finish and may not have a good fitting lid. These things make cooking more difficult.

Buying a Dutch oven is a life-time investment. We recommend spending the few extra dollars necessary to buy a really good quality Dutch oven such as "Lodge" brand. We believe you will be happier in the long run.

Some prefer the late entry on the scene, the aluminum Dutch oven. It is lighter in weight if you are considering packing weight. You can also buy square ones. They can be scrubbed out with soap or put in a dishwasher. However, on a fire, they are more prone to having "hot spots" and burning food, and they will not hold food as long or as well. But they do have certain advantages in some circumstances where weight is a factor.

SEASONING

Seasoning your cast iron Dutch oven prevents rust and makes your oven stick-free. It is the key to a good friendship with a new, or revitalized, Dutch oven.

To season your new Dutch oven the regular kitchen oven way use mild soapy water and wash your oven to remove the waxlike preservative put on by the manufacturer. Rinse and dry thoroughly. Using a good quality vegetable or salad oil, such as Wesson, oil all surfaces—both inside and out—with a cotton cloth. Add enough oil to cover the bottom of the Dutch oven and place it in a medium hot oven until the oil is hot, which will take about 30 minutes at 350 degrees. Remove the Dutch oven and carefully swab the oil all over the bottom and the sides. Add more oil and heat in a low oven (200 degrees) for one hour. Turn the oven off and leave it there overnight. In the morning, rub all surfaces with the remaining oil and wipe out what oil remains. Your new Dutch oven is now seasoned and ready for years of service.

Since this first method takes some time and often ends up with some smoke

 We've never had to do this with a Lodge oven, but some writers propose that if the lid doesn't seat well, smear valve grinding compound on the rim of the pot and the edge of the lid and rotate the lid until you have a good fit.

in the kitchen, there is another faster method to season your oven. This is the way the Kohlers do it.

Wash your new Dutch oven with soap and water, rinse thoroughly and dry to get rid of the preservative. Place your Dutch oven on the fire with about one-half inch of vegetable oil in it. When the oil gets hot, swirl it around in the Dutch oven to coat the bottom and the sides. You may want to use a cotton cloth. Pour out the excess oil and add more oil. Cook something in it that uses oil, such as chicken. Then clean the Dutch oven as described in the cleaning section of this book. Cook foods that use oil, or little water content, for one or two more times and that's all there is to it. Remember, the more you correctly use and clean your oven, the more seasoned and blacker it will get.

CLEANING

Cleanup is simple when you do it the right way. First, remove any excess food (if there should be a scrap left), and wipe out the "gungus" with a paper towel. Place the Dutch oven on the fire with the lid on. Heat the oven for a while and then crack the lid so that the moisture can escape. Leave the oven on the fire until everything inside is dry and black. This method works just like a self-cleaning oven at home. Don't let the oven stay on the fire beyond this point or it could overheat and warp a bit. You may have to rotate the oven to heat it evenly.

Remove your Dutch oven from the fire and scrape it out with a spatula or putty knife. Wipe it clean and then oil it inside and out, including the legs and handle, while the oven is still hot. Good tools and/or gloves come in handy during this whole process. You can complete this whole operation while you are visiting around the campfire with your family or friends and no one will hardly notice that you have done the dishes.

When done correctly, your oven will turn a uniform black with use. The Kohler ovens shine so much that they have been accused of painting their ovens with black spray paint.

If, for some reason, you get a sticky area in your oven, just reseason from step one. Wash it out with mild soap and water, rinse, then dry. While your oven is still warm, wipe it with oil as previously described. For normal use, never scour, use detergents on it, or put it in a dishwasher.

Should your Dutch oven get rusty, or the food you cook is discolored or has a metallic taste, you'll know that your oven has lost its seasoning and needs to be reseasoned. A wire brush or scouring pad will remove rust. Then follow the steps in the seasoning section and you are back in business.

Once you have your Dutch oven seasoned and "stick-proof," never lend it to anyone. The story goes, "lend your car, your lawnmower or your wife, but not your Dutch oven."

STORAGE

After your Dutch oven has been cleaned, oiled and cooled, store it in a warm, dry place. It is good to crack the lid so that air can circulate to the inside. A hook made from several layers of aluminum foil works good for this. A paper towel can be placed inside to absorb any moisture from the air.

Cast iron will break like glass if mistreated or dropped. Do not add cold water to a hot Dutch oven while cooking, it could easily cause your oven to crack.

DUTCH OVEN TOOLS

Having a few tools just for Dutch oven cooking sure makes the job more pleasant and easier. Find something to keep them in and keep them just for when you use your Dutch oven. A bucket, box, or wire milk crate works well. A set of good quality Dutch oven cooking tools will allow you to adjust the fire, place your Dutch oven in the fire, take it out, remove coals from the lid, remove the lid, and pour from the Dutch oven, without the worry or concern of being burned.

There are now on the market, lid holders for holding the lid of the Dutch oven and keeping it clean when it is not on the oven, and tote bags to cover your ovens while you get to and from your cooking site.

You need a shovel for placing coals, an ax for wood preparation and some long-handled barbecue tools are nice. We have extended the handles on regular kitchen tools to forty inches. Gloves, cotton rags and vegetable oil for cleaning your Dutch oven can also be kept in your box. A whisk broom to sweep coals off your Dutch oven before serving and when cleaning up really makes a difference.

FIRES AND TEMPERATURE CONTROL

There are many factors that influence the temperature inside your Dutch oven. You don't have to cook with high temperatures because of the design of the Dutch oven. Start out with moderate temperatures and work up. If you don't know exactly what is going on inside your Dutch oven, look and see. If it is too hot, remove some heat. If it is too cold, add some heat. Remember, "if you snooze, you lose."

The best kind of wood to use is what you have on hand. Keep in mind that the hard woods like fruit wood, oak and maple make much hotter coals than the softer woods like aspen, pine and poplar. This may affect your cooking times.

Wind can also greatly affect the temperature of your coals. A small breeze will heat the upwind side of your Dutch oven much hotter than the downwind side. To compensate for this, simply rotate your Dutch oven every once in a while.

Charcoal briquets give off a constant supply of heat and if you like the convenience of using them, go ahead. You'll need a slight air space between them and your Dutch oven. If you happen to have an indoor Dutch oven without legs you can use rocks, bricks or a little metal stand to set your Dutch oven on for better combustion of the briquets.

Altitude can also make a difference in how fast your meal will cook. If you are high in the mountains on that hunting or fishing trip, you will probably have to allow more cooking time than it takes in your backyard at a lower altitude.

Some scrap wood is okay for use in cooking, but you need to be careful because

 "A Dutch oven is probably the most versatile piece of cooking equipment available."   Dian Thomas in *Roughing It Easy*

some manufactured wood products contain a substance called Chromate-Copper-Arsenate (CCA) which gives off poisonous fumes when burned. Briquets are also noxious in a closed area so make sure you have adequate air circulation.

FIRE ARRANGEMENTS IN YOUR YARD

If you have a place in your backyard to make a fire pit, that's great. You can start simple with just one fire spot in your yard. You can use rocks around the outer edge just as you would in the mountains, or you can use a steel rim off an old wagon wheel, a piece of culvert, or build a fire pit by pouring concrete or set fire brick in sand or mortar.

You can make benches out of logs, or set pipe in concrete and add planks for seats around your fire pit. You could make this the central focus of a patio or put it off in a corner. By adding some round patio stepping stones in a few places around the pit, you can set your hot Dutch ovens out of the fire pit without killing your lawn.

When you outgrow a single fire pit, more can be added. The Kohler families each have three pits in their backyards. This allows versatility in cooking and increases the number of Dutch ovens that can be used. While a batch of biscuits are baking in one pit, a good fire can be kept going in another one for extra coals when needed or cooking additional dishes that can utilize more heat such as a good old-fashioned pot of stew.

If you don't have space or live in an apartment, you can make yourself a fire pan by cutting the end off a 55-gallon drum or cut it lengthwise and put some legs on it. You can build a fire in this anywhere. You can also use a metal wagon, a barbecue grill, a wheelbarrow or metal garbage can lid (with a little sand in it) to put your fire in. Recently, new Dutch oven cooking tables have come on the market that allow you to cook at a perfect height from the ground. These tables fold up for easy carrying and storage. Use Dutch ovens at home, in the park, at the beach, in the mountains or anywhere.

COOKING

We invite you to try all the recipes in this book. With a little practice, even the championship ones will become easy. Keep in mind that you can't take quality food out of your Dutch oven unless you put quality food into the recipe.

The best recipes for you to use in your Dutch oven are your own. Adapt any of them to your liking. Dutch oven cooking is usually never the same twice. Do your own thing, but remember, cook like a young bride that has a grouchy husband, work to make it right the first time.

Many things that are cooked in the Dutch oven are steamed. Steam is much hotter than boiling water, so things cook faster than you might think. They also taste better.

You can use garnishes and make your dishes very attractive for entertaining or just keep them simple.

Remember: Start with a moderate fire and work up.

Keep moisture in your Dutch oven.

Add only warm water when your oven is hot.

Enjoy yourself and share your experiences with others.

 The "lid lifter" tool is called a "gonch hook" in Spanish.

CHAPTER 2
Miscellaneous Cooking Helps

WHAT SIZE DUTCH OVEN?

Today, Dutch ovens are primarily found in the 8, 10, 12, 14 and 16 inch sizes and they run about 3 to 4 inches in depth. According to Lodge, the largest manufacturer of cast iron ware, the 12″ Dutch oven is the most popular size. There are larger and deeper sizes of Dutch ovens on the market, but make sure if purchasing these that the quality of cast and workmanship is good and that the walls are uniform in thickness to insure even cooking.

For your first Dutch ovens the 10″ and 12″ sizes are good. They are the most versatile. You can cook enough food to serve from 2-12 people. You will find your selection and sizes of Dutch ovens will increase to fit your needs the more you cook.

The chart below will give you some idea of how the various sizes are typically used:

Oven Size	Oven Capacity	Types of Food
8″	2 qts.	Recipes for two people, vegetables, desserts
10″	4 qts.	Anything for 2-6 people, beans, rolls, cobblers; good size for testing recipes
12″	6 qts.	Main dishes to serve 12-14 people, or side dishes of rolls, desserts
14″	8 qts.	Main dishes to serve 16-20 people, or side dishes of rolls, potatoes, vegetables
16″	14 qts.	Any food for large groups

HOLDING FOOD

When food is cooked, the best thing to do with it is to eat it. If this isn't possible for some reason, try these hints.

Breads   Remove from the Dutch oven and cover with a towel until ready to eat.

Cobblers   Remove from the heat and let stand in the Dutch oven.

Meats and Poultry	Keep some moisture in the Dutch oven and keep warm over a low fire. The meat will just get more tender.
Vegetables	Vegetables are better if not overcooked. Remove from the fire and then reheat just before serving. Don't add sauces or cheese until you are sure of the serving time.
Fish	Usually fish cooks so fast that you should wait until you are sure of your serving time before you start.

FIRE TEMPERATURES

Hand Method. To test the heat of your fire, hold the palm of your hand over the place in the fire where your food will be cooked. Count "one-and-one," and "two-and-two," and so on, for the seconds you can stand to hold your hand still. Move your hand around the fire surface to find the temperature you want.

If you are able to hold your hand for the counts listed below, the heat and temperature will be as follows:

Counts	Heat	Temperature
6 - 8	Slow	120°C - 175°C 250°F - 350°F
4 - 5	Moderate	175°C - 200°C 350°F - 400°F
2 - 3	Hot	200°C - 230°C 400°F - 450°F
1 or less	Very hot	230°C - 260°C 450°F - 500ºF

Briquets (Gives moderate to hot temperatures)

Dutch oven size	Number of coals on top	Number of coals on bottom
8"	6 - 8	4 - 6
10"	8 - 10	6 - 8
12"	10 - 12	8 - 10
14"	12 - 16	10 - 12
16"	16 - 18	12 - 16

When baking, you will want to use a higher ratio of briquets on the top, or you can remove the oven from the fire and continue to let it bake with just the coals on top.

USEFUL ACCESSORIES
Measuring spoon set
Measuring cup
Leather gloves
Shovel—some like the folding G.I. type

Dutch oven tools— you can make your own, but the TWIN-K set is the handiest
   one we've seen.
Long handled spoon—barbecue type
Long handled tongs—for moving briquets around
Spatula
Cooking oil in plastic container with screw lid
Cotton rag to wipe oil
Paper towels
Small whisk broom for removing ashes from the lid
Aluminum foil
Tin or aluminum pie plates
Pancake turner

HELPFUL DUTCH OVEN MEASURES
Dash= less than 1/8 teaspoon
3 teaspoons = 1 tablespoon
16 teaspoons = 1 cup
1 cup = ½ pint
2 cups = 1 pint
4 tablespoons = ¼ cup
5⅓ tablespoons = ⅓ cup
8 tablespoons = ½ cup
2 pints = 4 cups
         1 quart
4 quarts = 1 gallon
16 ounces = 1 pound

SERVING QUANTITIES FOR DUTCH OVEN PARTY
70 people (adult portions)

Potatoes	30 pounds of potatoes (three 14″ Dutch ovens)
	12 large onions
	3 pounds of cheese
	3 cubes of butter
Chicken	2 pieces of chicken per person (140 pieces)
	(two 16″ Dutch ovens, one 12″ Dutch oven)
Vegetables	12 large onions
(four 14″	4 heads of cauliflower
Dutch ovens)	4 bunches of broccoli
	24 carrots
	4 pounds of mushrooms
	4 pounds of cheese
	1 pound butter
	seasoning salt

Children under 10 usually eat ½ of an adult portion.

 *Seasoning it or breaking it in or "sweetening" your Dutch oven all describe
the act of cleaning, oiling and heating up the oven to make it nonstick.*

SAFETY

The most important factor for safety in cooking out-of-doors is the actions of the cook. Stop and think about possible accidents before they happen. Put on those gloves; make sure your Dutch oven doesn't slip while pouring hot oil from it. Keep small children away from the fire and hot Dutch ovens. Don't forget Dutch ovens stay hot for a long time. Children love to play with an ax, so if you are going to have it out, put it where tiny hands can't reach it.

In many of the national forests during the late summer and fall, open fires are prohibited. Please obey these rules. It's better to eat a cold sandwich than to start a forest fire. Remember, you are the most important safety device ever made.

"And one of the most valued pieces of equipment, toted all the way up the Missouri, across the Bitterroots and down the Columbia to the Pacific, and back home again, was a large-sized Dutch oven."
Don Holm reporting on the story of Lewis and Clark
Old-Fashioned Dutch Oven Cookbook

CHAPTER 3
Starting Out With Your Own Dutch Oven

THREE OLD FAVORITES

So you've got the itch to dazzle your family and friends with one of those scrumptious Dutch oven meals. You've got a couple of ovens and now you'd like to know where to begin. Well, the following three recipes selected by the Michauds, at least the kinds of food, are probably the most cooked ones in the business. Many a dutcher has started out with one, or all of the following, and has been hooked on the old, black pot ever since. Maybe it was on a scout outing, or at a family reunion, or at a church social, or maybe even on a river float that it was first attempted. Most likely, some of the ingredients didn't get added as per the recipe, or even made it at all, but chances are that it tasted great anyway. That's just the way the Dutch oven comes through and we're sure that it will for you too. Good luck!

DUTCH OVEN CHICKEN

2 chickens　　　　　　　　　　　*Fits in a 10" Dutch oven*
Flour
Seasoning

Skin and wash chicken parts. Coat in flour, salt and pepper mixture. To do this, put your seasonings and flour in a paper sack, add chicken parts and shake. Add approximately ½ inch of oil in the bottom of Dutch oven. Completely brown chicken parts. Remove from oven and drain off excess oil. Place chicken back in the Dutch oven and add approximately ¼ inch of warm water. Cover and place on a small bed of coals and steam for approximately 1 hour or until tender. Make sure there is always a small amount of moisture in the Dutch oven.

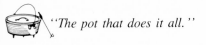*"The pot that does it all."*

Ted Trueblood, famed Western Editor
. for *Field and Stream* Magazine

DICK MICHAUD'S POTATOES, ONIONS AND BACON

1 large potato per person   *½ - 1 lb. of bacon*
½ onion per person   *Salt and pepper*

Cut the bacon into squares and line the bottom of a level Dutch oven. Cook until half done, then add the onions and then the potatoes. Slice the potatoes evenly at about ¼ inch. Cut the onions into sixths or eighths so they will break up readily while cooking. If you are trying to cook a lot of potatoes, heap them right to the brim because they will cook down about one-half. Salt and pepper more than you think is enough, put on the lid and set oven on the bed of coals. At this point, the old hands will say, "Don't check them until you can smell them." But, to begin with, go ahead and check them every 15 minutes. After each check, rotate your oven on the coals a quarter of a turn for even heat. When they are about half-cooked, you can turn them with a pancake turner to give each potato its turn on the bottom. Add a little bit of oil if needed, but not much. Cook until tender to the fork test. Generally about 45 minutes will do it, regardless of the size of the oven.

DUTCH OVEN COBBLER

2 cans of your favorite pie filling   *1 egg*
1 yellow cake mix   *Water or milk*

Use a 10″ Dutch oven. Pour your favorite filling (cherry, apple, blueberry, or any fruit you have canned is good) into the Dutch oven. Our favorites are cherry, huckleberry, apple and peach. We use a yellow cake mix. One-half package will make one 10″ Dutch oven cobbler. Add 1 egg and enough milk to make the batter the consistency of pancake batter. You may also use water if you prefer. Pour cake mixture on top of filling. Place lid on Dutch oven. Bake with coals on top and bottom for approximately 15 minutes. Remove oven from fire, and continue cooking from top only for an additional 10-20 minutes or until cobbler is done and golden brown.

CHAPTER 4

Meats, Poultry and Fish

STUFFED BEEF TENDERLOIN

This recipe prepared by David and Irene Johnson was adapted from the *Southern Living 1987 Annual Recipes,* a cookbook published by Oxmoor House.

14" Dutch oven
Serves 8-10

4 oz. frozen crab meat, cooked
1 2-4 lb. beef tenderloin, trimmed
1 tablespoon butter or margarine, melted
1½ teaspoons lemon juice
Garlic salt
Pepper, freshly ground
6 slices bacon, cut in half

½ cup sliced green onion
½ cup butter or margarine
½ cup white grape juice
⅛ teaspoon garlic salt
½ green pepper
½ red pepper

Place Dutch oven over coals and cook bacon slices until transparent. Store bacon slices for later use.

Trim excess fat from beef tenderloin. Cut tenderloin lengthwise in two different slits to within ½ inch of each end and bottom. Place crab (frozen or thawed) end to end inside tenderloin slits.

Melt 1 tablespoon butter on Dutch oven lid and combine with lemon juice; drizzle over crab. Fold top side of tenderloin over crab.

Tie tenderloin securely with heavy string at 2 inch intervals. Sprinkle outside of meat evenly with garlic salt and freshly ground pepper; place in Dutch oven.

Cook with coals on top and bottom of Dutch oven with a moderately high heat 40-60 minutes.

While meat is cooking, sauté green onion in ½ cup butter on Dutch oven lid. Add white grape juice and ⅛ teaspoon garlic salt. Cut 1 large green pepper and 1 large red pepper in half crosswise. Remove seeds and discard. Pour butter mixture into one of the halves of the green pepper and one of the halves of the red pepper.

After the meat is cooked, arrange bacon crosswise on the top of tenderloin. Put coals on lid of Dutch oven and cook for 5 minutes until bacon is crisp. For garnish, place pepper halves containing butter sauce on each side of tenderloin. Remove string, slice and serve.

DUTCH OVEN CHICKEN FANTASY

Lynn and Sue Packer brought their 20 years of Dutch oven experience to the Championship Day and took 1st Place. Just to prove what dutchers the Packers are, their last family wedding had a Dutch oven cookout instead of a wedding luncheon.

8-10 small chicken breasts, boned

Brown chicken breasts in ½ inch oil in 12″ Dutch oven, drain excess oil. Add ¼ cup water. Set aside.

In separate oven, combine the following:

1 cup maraschino cherry juice
½ teaspoon salt
1 cup brown sugar
¼ cup lemon juice or vinegar
1 tablespoon soy sauce
1 cup pineapple juice
¼ teaspoon paprika
½ teaspoon ginger
Juice from 1 small can of mandarin oranges
1 package Schilling dry sweet and sour mix
2 tablespoons cornstarch—to thicken

Bring to boil stirring constantly.

Add to above mixture:

1 cup pineapple chunks
½ cup green peppers, chopped
½ cup maraschino cherries
1 cup carrots, sliced
1 cup celery, diced
½ cup sweet, red onions
1 8-oz. can water chestnuts, sliced and drained
1 small can mandarin oranges

Pour over chicken. Steam for 1 hour on very low heat. Stir often.

TIMBERLINE CHICKEN

Pete Orton and Max Alleman first tried this recipe at their Timberline Boy Scout training session.

14" Dutch oven
Serves 12

2 broiler-fryers (2½ - 3 lbs. each) cut into pieces
2 teaspoons salt
½ teaspoon pepper
4 tablespoons shortening
3 8 oz. cans tomato sauce
3 tablespoons molasses vinegar
2 teaspoons liquid smoke flavoring
2 tablespoons instant minced onion
1 5 lb. bag briquets

In a small pan, combine the tomato sauce with the molasses vinegar, liquid smoke and instant onion; bring to a boil and simmer for 5 minutes. Set aside. (This sauce can be made several days ahead as it will keep well refrigerated.) Adjust to own taste.

Wash chicken pieces and pat dry. Sprinkle salt and pepper on all sides of the chicken pieces. Melt 4 tablespoons shortening, bacon drippings or salad oil in bottom of Dutch oven. Place about ½ of the chicken pieces in the bottom of the Dutch oven. Quickly brown on all sides and then remove. Brown remaining chicken pieces and replace all pieces together in Dutch oven. Pour the sauce over the chicken and place lid on top. Bake slowly for one hour with ⅓ of the coals on the bottom and ⅔ on the lid.

Delicious with 1 inch carrot slices baked with the chicken and served over rice, pasta or mashed potatoes.

BAKED ALASKAN SALMON "PARMESAN" VARIATION

Tyrone Lewis and Larry Lewis (no relation) took 2nd Place with their Baked Salmon. Truly, it was a marvelous sight when they took the lid off for the judges.

1 whole fresh or frozen salmon (3-4 lbs. without head)
4 tablespoons butter or margarine, softened and mixed
  with about 3 tablespoons of lemon juice
½ medium onion, sliced
½ lemon, sliced
Fresh parsley
6 ears corn on the cob, husked
6-8 cherry tomatoes
Parmesan cheese

Wash salmon and place on top of the 6 ears of corn which have been placed in bottom of 14″ Dutch oven. Season inside of salmon with salt, pepper and seasoned salt. Stuff with alternating slices of onion and lemon. Place 3 sprigs of parsley on stuffing.

Baste outside of salmon with butter and lemon oil. Add approximately 1 cup of water to oven and bake for approximately 20 minutes over medium coals. When fish is approximately three-quarters done, cut crosswise through skin and into meat (approximately ½ inch). Space cuts about 1½ inches apart. Open cuts and season with seasoned salt and sprinkle in Parmesan cheese.

Place 6 - 8 cherry tomatoes in oven with top quarter of tomato removed. Cover exposed top side of tomato with Parmesan cheese and allow these to bake for last 5-8 minutes. Serve with fish.

STUFFED PEPPER STEAK

Third Place on the Championship Day went to the two gals from Smithfield, Utah, Peggy Roskelley and Rosemary Parkinson. They really know their way around good cooking, in or out-of-doors.

1 large round steak

Cut into individual pieces and pound until thin. Sprinkle with coarse, ground pepper and rub in with palm of your hand.

Marinate for 4 - 6 hours in:

1 tablespoon tomato paste
1 teaspoon paprika
½ teaspoon garlic powder
1 cup soy sauce
¾ cup vinegar

Remove from marinade and apply layers of sliced green olives, chopped green peppers, chopped green onions and chopped mature mushrooms.

Roll as jelly roll and secure with toothpicks. Brown in a 12" Dutch oven in a small amount of oil. Remove Dutch oven from heat and pour 1 cup cooking sherry and 1 cup water over meat.

Return to fire and bake with coals on top and bottom for 1½ - 2 hours or until tender. Serve with rice and your favorite mushroom sauce.

Our Favorite Mushroom Sauce:

1 cup mature mushrooms, chopped
1 beef bouillon cube
⅔ cup water
2 tablespoons butter
2 tablespoons flour
½ cup sour cream
2 teaspoons Worcestershire sauce

Dissolve bouillon in water. Sauté mushrooms in butter. When done, add flour. Add bouillon mixture and stir constantly until thick. Fold in sour cream and Worcestershire sauce.

 "When the cook lifted the lid to turn the steaks, the odors escaping would whet the appetite of a dying man."
Ramon F. Adams in *Come and Get It*

DUTCH OVEN PACIFICA*

Ron Campbell and Al MacQueen were real competitors and imaginative dutchers. This beauty took 1st Place on Meat Day.

Shrimp
Salmon
Lobster
Clams
Scallops
Carrots
Peas
Rice
Shrimp sauce

Boil shrimp until done (about 5 minutes), then ice. Cook rice and remove when done and cook carrots and peas. Steam lobster, shrimp and clams approximately 15 minutes (don't overcook). Steam salmon approximately 10 minutes. Sauté scallops on lid.

Now make a bed of rice and peas in bottom of Dutch oven. Mound up various steamed clams, sautéed scallops, steamed shrimp and salmon. Arrange steamed carrots to make a "pleasing to the eye" arrangement. Put back on fire to warm.

Place ice in bowl and arrange chilled shrimp with sauce and serve.

* Use quantities appropriate to the size of your Dutch oven. Other fish may be substituted.

DUTCH OVEN CURRIED CHICKEN IN RICE PILAF, SOUTHERN STYLE

Brent Checketts and Richard Heiner were strong competitors every day. They were poetry in motion as they took 2nd Place on Meat Day with this delicious way to fix chicken.

2 medium sized chickens, cut up
½ cup flour
½ cup salad oil
3 - 4 garlic cloves, halved
4 medium onions, thinly sliced
1 cup chopped celery
2 medium bell peppers, chopped
Curry to taste
Salt to taste
2 cans tomatoes and juice
2 cups rice
1 cup raisins or currants
2 tablespoons butter or margarine
⅔ cup sliced almonds
Chopped parsley for garnish

Pilaf: One chopped onion in medium-hot 14″ Dutch oven, 2 tablespoons butter. Sauté onion until tender. Add rice, sauté 5-10 minutes. Add water just to cover rice, boil, reduce heat, cover, cook 35-40 minutes.

Curry: Coat chicken with flour. In medium-hot oven, brown chicken on all sides, remove from oven. In drippings, cook onions, celery, peppers, curry and salt until vegetables are tender. Stir in tomatoes and juice, add chicken. Heat to boiling; reduce heat, simmer 40 minutes or until chicken is tender.

Arrange rice in oven, with well in center. Spoon sauce and chicken pieces around center of rice.

Garnish with parsley, apple slices and browned sliced almonds.

BBQ CHICKEN

Val and Marie Cowley were a delight to have at the Cookoff. Talking with the spectators, cooking extra dishes in mountainman attire; they enjoy themselves anywhere. This version of chicken took 3rd Place on Meat Day for them.

1 small onion
1 small green pepper
2 tablespoons butter
2 tablespoons flour
¾ pint cider
1-2 teaspoons Worcestershire sauce
Dash of - ginger, allspice, cinnamon, cloves, dry mustard

2 tablespoons tomato ketchup
1-2 tablespoons honey
1 apple (peeled, cored, roughly chopped)
1 chicken
Flour (to coat chicken)

Finely chop onion and green pepper, add butter and sauté in 12″ Dutch oven. Add flour and cook for 1 minute. Stir in cider and bring to a boil. Add Worcestershire sauce, tomato ketchup, honey and apple. Add additional spices. Cover and simmer for 10 minutes. Set sauce aside.

Lightly flour chicken, place in Dutch oven with bacon and brown. Cover and simmer until almost done (about 1 hr). Cover chicken with sauce last 20 minutes of cooking time.

STEW *(With never fail gravy)*

Every Dutch oven cook has to have at least one good stew recipe. This is a possibility for you.

1 lb. stew meat
2 medium onions
Potatoes
Carrots

3 beef bouillon cubes
Browning sauce (Kitchen Bouquet)
3 cans cream of mushroom soup
¼ cup sugar

Heat ¼ inch oil in your 12″ Dutch oven. Brown stew meat and onions, then drain off the oil. Add potatoes, carrots and any other fresh vegetables you wish. Put in two or three beef bouillon cubes and two or three cans cream of mushroom soup plus enough warm water to cover the vegetables. Don't add any salt, but you can use any other seasonings you like. A little Kitchen Bouquet will make the gravy as brown as you like. Add ¼ cup of sugar to give your stew a unique flavor. You can cook this over a hot fire if you wish, but simmer until the vegetables are cooked, stirring occasionally.

DEEP FRIED FISH FILLETS

Even those people who don't like fish will founder on this recipe.

Fill your Dutch oven about one-third to one-half full of cooking oil and heat until lightly smoking. Cut the fillets into strips about 1½ inches wide and dip the fillets in a batter made of:

½ cup flour
1 teaspoon baking powder
½ teaspoon salt

½ cup cold water
1 egg white (beat until stiff and fold
into the above ingredients)

Place fillets in the heated oil and cook until golden brown. Serve piping hot.

GRAVY AND MEATBALLS

Add some Dutch oven biscuits to this and you've got a real meal.

2 - 2½ lbs. ground beef	Salt and pepper
2 eggs	Dry bread crumbs
½ cup catsup	1 package brown Herbal Gravy Mix
½ teaspoon rubbed sage	2 cans Golden Mushroom Soup

In a large bowl mix ground beef, eggs, catsup, onion soup mix, sage, salt and pepper to taste. Add enough dry bread crumbs to form small meat balls. Pour a little cooking oil into your 12 " Dutch oven and brown meatballs all over. Drain off any excess oil. Cover meatballs with 1 package Brown Herbal Gravy Mix prepared according to package instructions. Add 2 cans of Golden Mushroom Soup. Simmer with coals on bottom for 45 minutes or until done. Use very little salt.

PORK CHOPS AND POTATOES AND GRAVY

A simple recipe but don't make a "pig" out of yourself with it.

Add ⅛ inch oil to your Dutch oven and over hot coals brown your pork chops. Drain off excess oil and add sliced potatoes, onions and enough cream of mushroom soup mixed with about one-half of the water to cover the chops and potatoes. Simmer with coals on the bottom until the potatoes are tender.

ANYTIME STEW

An easy, quick anytime meal.

1 lb. stew meat	Mushrooms
2 large onions	Cauliflower
Potatoes	Broccoli
Carrots	Seasonings
Beef bouillon cube	Cornstarch and water
Kitchen Bouquet	

Put ¼ inch of oil in your 12 " Dutch oven and place on fire. When oil is hot add stew meat and 2 onions cut in quarters, cook until meat is browned. Drain off excess oil. Cut vegetables to desired size. Carrots should be cut smaller because they take longer to cook. Add potatoes, carrots, mushrooms, cauliflower, broccoli or any other vegetables of your choice. Season with salt, pepper, curry powder, oregano, cloves or any other seasonings you desire. Add enough warm water to cover vegetables, add one bay leaf and one bouillon cube. Place on fire, cook until vegetables are tender. When vegetables are tender, thicken broth with flour or cornstarch and water mixture. Add a browning sauce (Kitchen Bouquet) if a browner gravy is desired. Excellent served with Dutch oven rolls.

"It is as difficult for me to imagine a river trip without a Dutch oven as it would be to imagine one without a raft, kayak, canoe, or peanut butter."
Patricia Chambers in *River Runners' Recipes*

SWISS STEAK COUNTRY STYLE

Round steaks never tasted so good as in this recipe of Mike Kohlers.

Round steak (cut into
    individual portions)
Cream of Mushroom Soup

Kitchen Bouquet
Seasonings to taste

(Use 10, 12, or 14" Dutch oven, depending on size of group).

Brown round steak in small amount of oil in Dutch oven (no salt). Remove excess oil and add cream of mushroom soup diluted with water. Add browning sauce (Kitchen Bouquet) for color and simmer in Dutch oven for 1 hour or until steaks are tender. Cook from bottom only. If you like onion flavor, brown onions along with steaks.

SAUSAGE AND CABBAGE

This one always gets good reviews at the Kohler's Dutch oven workshops even though it's so simple to make.

1 large head of cabbage
½ cube of butter
Seasonings to taste

1 large sausage
Water

Clean and wedge one large head of cabbage (remove core), place in a 12" Dutch oven. Season to taste (seasoned salt, butter, salt and pepper). Place one large Polish sausage on top of cabbage, add a small amount of water to the bottom of Dutch oven and steam until tender over medium coals from bottom only (approximately 30-45 minutes). Excellent served with cornbread.

SON-OF-A-GUN STEW

Back in the old days, they called this stew a slightly different name which we won't mention here. But then it also had some left-over parts of a cow in it which we won't mention either. Anyway, Val and Marie Cowley's recipe looks fine to us.

½ lb. bacon
2 lbs. cubed beef (may be round, 7-bone roast, blade or chuck roast)

1 lb. carrots
2 lbs. potatoes
2 green peppers
¾ cup soy sauce
Tabasco (optional)

5 medium stalks celery
2 medium onions
4 cups whole bottled tomatoes
½ cup Worcestershire sauce

Fry bacon in 12" Dutch oven. Add onions and meat. Sauté until brown. Add vegetables and seasonings. Cover and simmer about 1 hour or until vegetables are tender.

BARBECUE CHICKEN CORDON BLEU WITH POTATO LOGS

Deloy Gardner and son, Ron, and one of their good, solid eating recipes.

2 oz. Parmesan cheese	*Pepper*
1 tablespoon paprika	*Thyme*
4 whole chicken breasts, halved	*¼ cup melted butter*
8 thin slices cooked ham	*½ cup barbecue sauce*
4 slices Swiss cheese	*4 potatoes cut in quarters*
Salt	

Skin and bone chicken breasts. Place each half between sheets of plastic wrap and pound meat with mallet until ⅛ inch thick. Layer chicken, ham, and Swiss cheese and roll jellyroll style. Dip in melted butter and place in 12″ Dutch oven, then add potatoes and bake with coals on top and bottom for approximately 40 minutes. Baste with butter, barbecue sauce, salt, pepper, and thyme mixture. Garnish with Parmesan cheese and paprika before serving.

DUTCH OVEN STEAK DINNER

Try this recipe for a full meal dinner.

Serves 4-6 people

12″ Dutch oven

2-3 lbs. top round	*2 sticks of celery*
or sirloin steak	*2 cups tomato juice*
4 large potatoes	*1 teaspoon salt*
4 carrots	*1 tablespoon sugar*
1 large onion	*4 tablespoons minute tapioca*

Cut the steak into pieces and brown in a 12″ Dutch oven with small amount of oil. Drain off excess oil and add potatoes, cut into chunks, sliced carrots, celery and onion. Mix the tomato juice, salt, sugar and tapioca and pour over the meat and vegetables.

Bake over medium coals for approximately 1½ hours or until meat is tender.

To keep your Dutch oven from getting lost, take a "punch-out" from an electrical box, put your initials on it with a stamp or engraving tool, and fasten one to the lid and one to the pot with "S" rings.

BBQ STUFFED MEATLOAF

Marcia Craw Moss, Kathy Hogan and a tasty main dish.

Mix together:
4 lbs. ground beef
2 cups oatmeal
4 eggs
3 tablespoons Worcestershire sauce

Dice:
1 large sweet onion
1 small green pepper (optional)
8 oz. mushrooms
1 garlic clove

Grate:
1½-2 cups cheese

Place a large strip of Saran Wrap on a flat surface. Pat meat out and put another piece of Saran Wrap on top, then use rolling pin to roll it out to a rectangle about ½ inch thick. (Using rolling pin over Saran Wrap prevents sticking.) Place diced vegetables and cheese on top of rectangle after removing top layer of Saran Wrap. Roll meat and vegetables as you would a cinnamon roll. Use bottom layer of Saran Wrap to help you roll and form its shape. Place in a foil-lined 12″ Dutch oven, seam down. Bend to fit if needed. Bake for 15-20 minutes and baste with barbecue sauce. Bake for additional 15-20 minutes and baste again. Bake for approximately 1½-2 hours (total cooking time) with coals on top and bottom.

Serve with new potatoes and broccoli. Garnish with sliced, sautéed mushrooms and parsley.

Barbecue Sauce:
2 8 oz. cans tomato sauce
½ cup brown sugar
2 tablespoons cornstarch
1 teaspoon dry mustard
½ teaspoon cloves, garlic powder and onion powder
¼ teaspoon allspice
2 tablespoons Worcestershire sauce

Mix together — simmer until it starts to thicken.

DUTCH OVEN BEEF STROGANOFF

Wynn and Cecelie Costley and an interesting meat dish.

½ lb. bacon	1 cup sour cream
3 lbs. steak	1 teaspoon celery seed
1 medium onion	½ teaspoon sage
2 cloves garlic	2 cups rice
1½ lbs. mushrooms	Salt and pepper
½ cup chives	Parsley

Cut bacon and steak into bite-size pieces. Brown meats well (about 45 minutes) in a 12″ Dutch oven. Add chopped onion and garlic to meat and sauté. Add enough water to cover meat and simmer for 2½ hours over low fire, checking water level at times. Add 2 cups rice and chopped chives. Cook 30 more minutes or until rice is tender. Then add sliced mushrooms, sour cream, and parsley.

DUTCH OVEN BEEF

Low and Ada Gardner came down from their dude ranch in Smoot, Wyoming to participate in the Cookoff. They use the cast iron ovens most every day of their business year in cooking for their friends who come to the ranch. They were a special couple and everyone was their friend before they left. They buried their entry to cook it. Of course everyone had to come over and rubberneck that operation which is part of what the Cookoff is all about.

Round roast, 15 pounds
1 onion
Seasoned salt
Seasoned pepper
Kitchen Bouquet

Dig a pit big enough to be 10 inches larger than Dutch oven. Build a fire in the pit and to the side. Brown the meat in the Dutch oven. Use Kitchen Bouquet if needed. Slice onion over meat and sprinkle with salt and pepper. Do not add moisture.

Rim the Dutch oven with a 4 inch strip of aluminum foil to keep ashes out of the meat. Place Dutch oven in pit and shovel remainder of coals around and over Dutch oven. Cover with dirt and seal completely, making sure that no smoke is escaping. This can be buried the night before, early in the morning or 6 hours before eating.

BARBECUED SPARERIBS

Nothing juicier comes out of a black pot than ribs . . . hhhmmmmmmm.

Spareribs or pork fingers (boneless)
Barbecue sauce

This can be cooked in any size Dutch oven you desire.

When cooking any meat entree, it is suggested that ½ lb. of meat be cooked for each person to be served.

Brown in hot oil the number of country style spareribs or pork fingers desired. Drain off excess oil. Add your favorite barbecue sauce, making sure all meat is covered. Simmer 1½ - 2 hours or until tender on warm bed of coals, cooking from bottom only.

BAR-B-QUE

For a family outing up the canyon, this dish will make a hit with everyone.

Over a hot fire in a 12″ Dutch oven brown 3 lbs. of hamburger and 1 large chopped onion. When the hamburger is completely browned, remove excess fat and add 1 pint catsup, 1 pint tomato juice and salt and pepper to taste. Bring mixture to boil and thicken with 2-3 tablespoons of flour dissolved in a small amount of water. Add 1 tablespoon of Worcestershire sauce, 1 teaspoon of curry powder. Simmer over a medium fire for approximately 2-3 hours. Serves approximately 25.

BAKED CHICKEN AND RICE

Chicken and Dutch ovens seem to go together. This is an easy, but tasty version by Wallace Kohler.

1 cup rice
1 chicken
1 package dry Lipton Onion Soup Mix
1 can chicken broth
1 can cream of mushroom soup
Water

Pour rice (not cooked) into a 10″ Dutch oven. Place cut up chicken parts on top of the rice. Sprinkle Lipton Onion Soup Mix on top of the chicken. Dilute chicken broth and cream of mushroom soup with 1 can water. Pour this mixture over the chicken and bake with coals on top and bottom for at least one hour.

CHICKEN CORDON BLEU

You may pay more for Cordon Bleu in a fancy restaurant in the big city, but it won't taste as good as this cooked up in your backyard.

Use one chicken breast per serving

Skin and bone chicken breasts. Place each breast between 2 pieces of waxed paper and pound until it's ¼ inch thick. Take a thin slice of ham and a thin slice of Swiss cheese and layer; chicken, ham, and then cheese; then roll tightly. Place the rolls in your Dutch oven and cover them with a mixture of two parts cream of chicken soup and one part milk. Don't add any salt. You may add a teaspoon of lemon juice if you wish. Cook with coals on both top and bottom for the first 15 minutes, then another 45 minutes with coals on top of your Dutch oven. Add garnishes and serve.

CORNISH GAME HENS

This is probably the most delectable looking pot's worth at the Kohler's workshops. You won't believe it till you see it all ready to eat.

Wash and stuff 4 game hens with your favorite stuffing. Place stuffed hens on a rack in a 12″ Dutch oven. Baste with your favorite basting sauce or glaze. Two of our favorites are included. Add a small amount of warm water. Place Dutch oven on hot coals and cook from bottom only for 15-20 minutes. Add coals to top and continue cooking for approximately 40-45 minutes or until game hens are fully cooked and golden brown. If leg joints move freely, hens should be done. If hens are browning too quickly, remove some or all coals from top of Dutch oven and cook from bottom only. While cooking, remove lid and baste frequently. For a complete meal add carrots, potatoes, onion, cauliflower, broccoli and mushrooms around hens. If you are cooking game hens only, 6 will fit in a 14″ Dutch oven.

Basting Sauce
Proportions are:
¼ water
½ vinegar
¼ butter or vegetable oil
1 teaspoon Worcestershire sauce (more for larger quantities)
Dash of salt

Glaze
⅓ cup melted butter
¼ cup canned condensed consommé
¼ cup light corn syrup

PHEASANT — PARTRIDGE

This and the next two recipes are several of Wallace Kohler's favorite "fowl" dishes. They are also easy to do and great to eat.

Remove bones and slice all the meat in ⅛ inch slices. Add some oil to your Dutch oven and cook meat until tender (it will turn white). Drain off excess oil and add sliced fresh or frozen vegetables such as peas, carrots, etc. Cover with cream of chicken soup and simmer with coals on the bottom until the vegetables are cooked. Use very little salt.

STIR-FRY CHICKEN

Cut chicken breasts into thin strips. Add green onions, cut celery on a diagonal, French cut green beans, cut carrots in strips (julienne style), and cut mushrooms in quarters. Stir-fry in peanut oil in your Dutch oven over hot coals. Add other items as desired such as slivered almonds, water chestnuts, pea pods, soy sauce, etc.

DEEP-FRIED CHICKEN

This recipe is for those who don't have to worry about all that oil and like their chicken crispy.

Fill your Dutch oven about one-third to one-half full of oil and heat it until the oil is lightly smoking. You will probably want to have some flames around your Dutch oven for this.

Roll cut-up chicken pieces in flour seasoned with salt and pepper. Fry the chicken until it is golden brown, stirring once or twice. When cooked, remove the chicken from the oil. This will only take about one-half hour.

SWEET AND SOUR PORK

Richard Heiner and Brent Checketts,the old pros, produced this gourmet treat. When you start feeling like you can tackle anything in a Dutch oven, try this one.

2½ lbs. lean pork chops
¼ cup soy sauce
1½ tablespoons dry sherry
2 teaspoons sugar
1 egg yolk
10 tablespoons cornstarch
3 cups vegetable oil
1 large yellow onion
8 green onions
1 red or green pepper
1 oz. mushrooms
2 stalks celery
1 medium cucumber
3 tablespoons vegetable oil
1 can (20 oz.) pineapple chunks in syrup
¼ cup white vinegar
3 tablespoons tomato sauce
1 cup water

Mix soy sauce, sherry, sugar, and egg yolk in a large glass bowl. Mix in pork. Cover and let stand 1 hour, stirring occasionally.

Drain pork, reserving soy sauce mixture. Coat pork with 8 tablespoons of the cornstarch. Heat the 3 cups oil in a 12" Dutch oven over high fire. Cook one-half of the pork in oil until brown, about 5 minutes. Drain on absorbent paper. Cook and drain remaining pork.

Cut yellow onion into thin slices. Remove seeds from pepper and chop coarsely. Clean mushrooms and cut into halves or quarters. Cut celery into ½ inch slices. Cut cucumber into ¼ inch wide pieces.

In your Dutch oven heat the 3 tablespoons oil over hot fire. Add all the prepared vegetables to oil. Stir-fry 3 minutes. Drain pineapple, reserving syrup. Add the syrup, reserved soy sauce mixture, vinegar and tomato sauce to vegetables. Combine water and remaining 2 tablespoons cornstarch. Add to vegetables. Cook and stir until sauce boils and thickens. Add pork and pineapple. Cook and stir until hot throughout. Makes 6 servings.

"If there is anything that can't be cooked in a Dutch oven, I don't know what it is."

Don Holm in the *Old Fashioned Dutch Oven Cookbook*

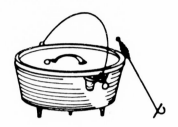

"Old Black Magic"

If there's anything blacker than a Dutch oven,
  It seems to escape my seeking mind.
But a better meal than comes from them,
  Would be most difficult to find.

For nearly any possible occasion,
  Any time, any place or which-ever meal,
Get out the black Dutch ovens
  And cook up a scrumptious deal.

If you're doing breakfast in the canyon,
  Or your backyard or by a cool lake,
Try "All-In-One"; potatoes, ham, onion and eggs,
  And then let the Dutch oven bake.

At a good old-fashioned family reunion,
  Or when the neighborhood comes to dine,
Fill up several black Dutch ovens
  And be prepared for a wonderful time.

Try one full of barbecued pork fingers,
  and every now and then
Do one full of the elegant,
  plump, juicy, stuffed Cornish hen.

Oh! There's many things to choose from!
    Dutch oven chicken and rolls at least,
Then potatoes with onions and fruit cobbler.
    And there's a real tasty feast.

Cook up a Dutch oven full of vegetables
    With melted cheese a seeping through;
Or do a batch of cornbread, cinnamon rolls,
    A huckleberry pie or a beef stew.

Wanting something on the plainer side,
    Try baked beans and sourdough bread;
Or be a little bit more versatile
    And try a genuine pizza instead.

Through winter storms when power fails
    Don't bemoan your miserable fate,
With your fireplace and "Old Black Magic"
    You can cook for family or a date.

When Dutch oven cooking over coals so hot and red,
    Let us give you a kindly clue,
Second helpings are in style
    Or, a third or a fourth if you'd like too.

Now ere this appetizing poem
    Comes to its destined end,
Keep your "Dutch Ovens" black and clean
    And they will be your life-time friend.

Eleanor A. Kohler

PRAIRIE STEW

Tom Hatch claims the secret to Dutch oven cooking is to keep it simple and old fashioned. At the Cookoff, Tom used sage brush for his heat source.

12" Dutch oven
Serves 15 people

3 lbs. good grade cubed beef
2 medium cans of tomatoes
1 large can of tomato juice

Vegetables:

Onions
Celery
Parsley
Carrots (easy on the carrots)
Whole corn (mostly for color)

Broccoli
Cabbage (don't forget)
Potatoes
Peas

Butter
Worcestershire sauce
Ketchup
Salt and pepper

Braise meat until well done. Add tomatoes, tomato juice, celery, and onions. Simmer for 21 minutes. Add remaining vegetables starting with vegetables which require the longest cooking time (potatoes and carrots). Keep waking it up (stirring) as the stew cooks. It is not what is in the stew but how it is made. It should be against the law to use canned vegetables. (except for the tomatoes). A shot of butter, Worcestershire sauce, ketchup, plus salt and pepper is all the kick it needs. Stew is better overcooked than undercooked.

CHAPTER 5
Vegetables

DUTCH OVEN STIR-FRY VEGETABLES WITH CHICKEN

Mike and Juanita Kohler's son Dennis says this recipe of his is, "A culmination of the culinary art with mystic appeal to the most discerning of tastes."

12" Dutch oven
Serves 6-8 people

1½ lbs. skinless, boneless chicken breasts
(cut into 1 inch pieces)
3 tablespoons vegetable oil
3 cups broccoli florets
8 oz. fresh mushrooms, sliced
4 green onions (use entire onion, sliced)
3 carrots (peeled and sliced)

2 cups cauliflower florets
3 stalks celery, sliced
½ cup soy sauce
½ cup apple juice
½ teaspoon fresh ground ginger
1 clove garlic (minced)
1 tablespoon corn starch
dissolved in ¼ cup water

Marinate chicken in soy sauce, apple juice and garlic for 15-20 minutes prior to cooking. Reserve marinade for later use. In your Dutch oven heat oil to medium hot. Add chicken and stir-fry for 3 minutes until chicken becomes opaque. Remove from oven and set aside. In your Dutch oven combine the broccoli, carrots, cauliflower and celery. Stir-fry for 3-4 minutes. Add mushrooms, onions, and ginger. Stir fry for 3-4 more minutes. Add dissolved corn starch, reserved marinade and chicken. Cook until heated through and sauce has thickened. Serve immediately. This recipe is also excellent served with long grain white rice.

SAVORY RICE AND MUSHROOMS — KAMPIN' KITCHEN STYLE

Don and Mariem Emmer from San Fernando, California shared this recipe with us.

12" Dutch Oven
Serves 10-12 People

2 cups Uncle Ben's Rice
2 tablespoons parsley flakes
2 teaspoons salt
1 tablespoon garlic powder
2 tablespoons butter/margarine
8 oz. canned sliced mushrooms

3 tablespoons onion flakes
3 tablespoons vegetable flakes
1 teaspoon Italian seasoning
5 chicken bouillon cubes
5½ cups hot water

Spray cold oven with Pam, blend dry seasonings together with dry rice. Put in oven. Dissolve bouillon cubes in hot water, stir in butter or margarine, then pour over rice mix. Maintain 8-10 coals under oven and 15-18 coals on lid until just boiling, then reduce coals to 6-8 under oven, 12-15 on lid, to keep mixture at a simmer. Drain mushrooms and stir into rice. Continue to simmer until most of water is absorbed. Remove from heat a few minutes before serving and fluff with a fork. Approximate cooking time 35 minutes.

SUMMER GARDEN DELIGHT

This bouquet of summer garden vegetables was the Championship Day side dish for 1st place winners Lynn and Sue Packer.

1 cup potatoes
1 cup carrots
1 cup cauliflower
1 cup broccoli
1 cup onions
1 cup mushrooms
Spike brand seasoning (39 natural herbs and spices)
Salt to taste

Add ¼ inch of water and steam in 12" Dutch oven over low fire for approximately 40 minutes. Add 2 cups grated American processed cheese before serving.

DUTCH OVEN POTATOES AND ONIONS

This 2nd Place finisher is a delicious Dutch oven potato recipe by Tyrone Lewis and Larry Lewis.

In 12″ Dutch oven, cook ½ lb. cut up bacon until crisp. Add ¼ inch vegetable oil, then add 12 sliced potatoes and 6 equal sized sliced onions. Add ½ lb. butter and lots of salt and pepper. Stir every 5 - 10 minutes (depending on how hot the coals are).

When ¾ done, drain excess oil and add 1 can cream of mushroom soup. When done, sauté 2 lbs. fresh mushrooms on bottom of Dutch oven lid. Cover potatoes with sharp cheddar cheese and add mushrooms. Serve.

GREEN BEANS WITH TOMATO TOPPER

Peggy Roskelley and Rosemary Parkinson have a way with vegetables as is proven by their 3rd Place winner in that category for the Championship Day.

Wash and snip fresh green beans. Place in steamer basket in 12″ Dutch oven. Salt lightly and add about ½ cup water to Dutch oven. Put lid on and steam over hot coals about 30 minutes.

Tomato Topper
½ cup butter or margarine, softened
¼ cup finely chopped tomatoes
Dash of chopped fresh dill
Dash of pepper

Mix together and serve mixed with the green beans.

WHOLE WHEAT VEGETARIAN PIE

Dean Hatch from Southern California and his alternating partners of wife Julie, or son Jay, do unbelievable things with a Dutch oven. This pie can really be classed as gourmet level work. Try it some time when you really want to test your skills and amaze your friends.

1 cup whole wheat flour	1 15 oz. can tomato sauce
1 cup all-purpose flour	½ cup green beans, cooked and cut
1 teaspoon salt	½ cup whole kernel corn, cooked
⅔ cup shortening	1 tablespoon brown sugar
5-7 tablespoons Egg Vinegar Water*	1 teaspoon dried oregano, crushed
1 cup chopped celery	½ teaspoon chili powder
½ cup carrots, shredded	½ teaspoon salt
½ cup fresh mushrooms, sliced	¼ teaspoon dried basil, crushed
½ cup green peppers, chopped	¼ teaspoon pepper
½ cup zucchini, chopped	¼ teaspoon ground allspice
1 clove garlic, minced	1 cup cheddar cheese, shredded
1 tablespoon cooking oil	1 egg, beaten

* Egg Vinegar Water (This has been used for over 100 years) Beat egg lightly in a 1 ½ cup measure, add 1 tablespoon vinegar and fill cup with cold water so that you have a total of 1 ½ cups of liquid. Store what you do not use for future use.

Stir together flours and 1 teaspoon salt, cut in shortening until pieces are the size of small peas. Sprinkle egg vinegar water, 1 tablespoon at a time, tossing mixture after each addition. Form into a ball. Roll half of the pastry to ⅛ inch thickness and fit into a 9 inch pie plate.

In 12″ Dutch oven cook zucchini, celery, carrot, mushrooms, green peppers and garlic in hot oil until tender (10 charcoals under the oven). Add tomato sauce, beans, corn, sugar and seasonings. Simmer, uncovered 5 minutes (6 charcoals under the oven). Spoon vegetable mixture into shell, sprinkle with cheese. Roll out remaining pastry. Adjust top crust; seal edge and crimp. Cut vents in top pastry.

Beat egg and 1 tablespoon water together then brush over crust. Bake in 350⁰ oven 20 minutes with foil on edge of crust (12-14 charcoals under oven and 10-12 charcoals on top). Remove foil and bake 20-25 minutes. Let stand 10-15 minutes before serving to 6 friends.

 Check recipes ahead—have all nuts chopped, sauces mixed, chocolate or butter melted, seasoning mixed. etc.

VEGETABLE PIE

Peggy Roskelley and Rosemary Parkinson knocked the judges' eyes out with this 1st Place winner on the Vegetable Day. The recipe doesn't mention it, but they peeled and sculpted a tomato "rose" and put it on the pie after it was cooked. Classy.

Enough pastry for a two-crust pie
¾ lb. mushrooms, sliced
1 large onion, chopped
1 green pepper, diced
2 yellow squash, sliced
2 zucchini, small, diced
2 tomatoes, peeled and sliced
½ cup grated Parmesan and Monterey Jack cheese
¼ lb. grated cheddar cheese
1½ cups mayonnaise
⅓ cup butter
Dash of garlic salt

Roll out pie dough big enough to fit bottom of 12" Dutch oven and up the sides 1½ inches.

Sauté mushrooms, onions, green peppers, squash and zucchini in the butter. Cook until crisp. Place sliced tomatoes on top of crust in Dutch oven.

Mix cheese together and sprinkle one cup of mixture on top of tomatoes. Cover this with vegetables. Sprinkle with garlic. Mix remaining cheese with the mayonnaise and spread over top. Bake using medium heat with coals on both top and bottom for 10 minutes, then remove coals from the bottom. Bake until the top is a golden brown.

CHEESY POTATO WEDGES

These go great with fresh trout, according to Wallace and Pat Kohler.

12" Dutch oven
Serves 4-6

Ingredients:
4 Russet potatoes
½ cube butter
⅓ cup Parmesan cheese
½ teaspoon garlic powder
1 teaspoon seasoned salt
Parsley flakes

Wash potatoes and cut each one into 8 wedges. Melt butter in Dutch oven. Coat potato wedges with butter on both sides and arrange in the Dutch oven in a circular pattern. Mix cheese and spices and sprinkle over the potatoes. Sprinkle with parsley flakes and bake with ⅓ of the coals on the bottom and ⅔ of them on the top until you can pierce the potatoes easily with a fork. Watch the bottom heat, you may have to finish baking just from the top. Don't overcook.

VEGETABLE LASAGNA

A unique approach to this recipe by 3rd Place winners on Vegetable Day, Val and Marie Cowley.

1 quart tomatoes	*¾ teaspoon oregano, crumbled*
1 quart tomato sauce	*¾ teaspoon basil, crumbled*
2 large onions, chopped	*⅛ teaspoon black pepper*
1 small clove garlic, minced	*1½ tablespoons oil*
¾ lb. mushrooms, chopped	*1 lb. pkg. lasagna noodles*
5 carrots, chopped	*2 lbs. cottage cheese*
2 green peppers, chopped	*1 lb. mozzarella cheese, grated*
5 oz. Parmesan cheese	

Combine vegetables in 12" Dutch oven and sauté in oil until tender. Add tomatoes, sauce and spices. Simmer 10 minutes. Remove ½ of vegetable mixture into bowl. Cover remaining mixture with layer of cooked noodles. Spoon layer of cottage cheese over noodles and sprinkle with mozzarella. Repeat with noodles and cheese until gone. Pour remainder of mixture over noodles. Sprinkle with Parmesan cheese and bake with coals on top and bottom for 1 hour or until bubbling hot.

DELUXE POTATOES

Here's a different approach to the potato in a black iron pot. Really yummy.

6 medium cooked and shredded potatoes	*¼ cup butter*
2 cans cream of chicken soup	*1 cup sour cream*
1 cup mayonnaise	*⅓ cup green onions*
1½ cups grated cheddar cheese	*2 cups corn flakes*

Mix together all of the above ingredients (except corn flakes). Place in a well greased 10" Dutch oven. Top with crushed corn flakes. Bake in a moderate fire from top and bottom until heated thoroughly, approximately 30-35 minutes.

VEGETABLES ALA KOHLERS

This is the workshop recipe by the Kohlers. Folks just won't leave this dish alone. *This recipe can be used in any size Dutch oven.*

Cut up and mix equal parts of fresh broccoli, cauliflower, carrots, onions (small white pearl onions are excellent), and mushrooms or any of your favorite vegetables. Season with salt, pepper and your favorite seasonings. Add several pats of butter and a small amount of water. Steam until tender over hot coals. Check often to make sure there is always some water in Dutch oven. When vegetables are tender, drain off excess moisture. Add about 2 cups grated cheese to top of vegetables, replace lid. Ready to serve when cheese has melted. A helpful tip is to use a baster to remove excess moisture from Dutch oven before adding cheese. If you use pearl onions, a good tip is to blanch them in hot water and then slip the skins off. This saves a lot of time trying to peel each onion.

DUTCH OVEN FRENCH PEAS

A succulent dish from Marcia Craw Moss, Kathy Hogan and Jane Gyllenskog. Cut 8 slices of bacon into ½ inch pieces and fry in 12" Dutch oven until crisp.

Add and cook 1 minute: *4 cups finely shredded lettuce*
8 green onions sliced (pearl onions can be used)

Stir in: *4 tablespoons flour*

Add 2 cups chicken broth and cook until thick, stirring constantly. Add 4 pkgs. (10 oz. each) frozen peas, 2 cans (5 oz.) water chestnuts, drained and sliced, and 1 teaspoon salt.

Place lid on Dutch oven and cook for 10 minutes. Use 5-8 briquets on top and bottom. Keep heat low. Serve and enjoy!

CORN COBLETS AND POTATOES

Shelley Johnson brought this recipe to the Cookoff from Rexburg, Idaho.

Melt ⅛ cup Crisco in bottom of 12" Dutch oven. Put in layer of sliced potatoes (¼ inch thick). Salt and pepper. Add a few sliced onions. Next layer is 2 inch lengths of well-buttered coblets of corn.

Add another layer of potatoes and onions. Top with salt and pepper. Place over white coals (about 18-20) on the bottom and (9-12) on the top. Cook for 35-40 minutes. Remove from heat, keeping coals on top of lid for 5 minutes longer. Remove the coals from top of lid. Remove lid and drizzle ¼ cup melted butter over top of layers. Let set for 2 minutes, then serve.

CREAMED CARROTS, PEAS AND ZUCCHINI

Any respectable vegetable section should have at least one recipe to help the reader handle all those zucchini from just the one hill! Here's a tasty answer from Dick and Pat Michaud for the annual problem.

2 small unpeeled zucchini, sliced
8 small carrots
1 cup peas
3 tablespoons butter
3 tablespoons all-purpose flour
4 tablespoons nonfat dry milk

Cook carrots in one 8" Dutch oven in boiling salt water for about 15 minutes; add zucchini and peas for last 5 minutes. Drain; reserving liquid. Melt butter in second 8" Dutch oven; remove from heat and stir in flour. Mix nonfat dry milk with enough carrot, pea, zucchini liquid to make one cup milk. Add to second Dutch oven and cook over low heat, stirring constantly, until thickened. Add carrots, peas and zucchini and heat until all is hot. Serves 4-6.

 "To John Simpson—one Dutch oven—$4.00"
Bill of sale on John Colter's property—1813.

DUTCH OVEN GARDEN DELIGHT

Errol and Le Nielson adapted this recipe from a delightful young couple of Dutch oven cooks who ran a river floating outfitting/guide operation in Idaho.

12" Dutch oven
Serves 8-10

Ingredients:

1 lb. white rice	*1 cup broccoli, diced*
1 cup tomato, diced	*1 medium can black olives, sliced*
1 cup onion, diced	*2 cans cream of mushroom soup*
1 cup green pepper, diced	*5 cans water*

Mix all ingredients in Dutch oven, being sure the soup is dissolved. Place 10-12 briquets under oven and 12-15 on lid. After ½ hour, stir every 15 minutes. This will take from 1-1½ hours to cook. You may need to add another cup of water the last 15-30 minutes of cooking.

ORIENTAL VEGETABLES

An original recipe by Ron Gardner and Steven D. Murdoch.

12" Dutch oven
Serves 12

Ingredients:

2 cups rice	*1 cup bean sprouts*
4 cups water	*½ cup peanut oil*
1 carrot, thinly sliced	*2 cups water*
1 stalk celery, sliced	*¼ cup soy sauce*
1 small can bamboo shoots	*½ teaspoon ginger*
1 green pepper, diced	*1 tablespoon brown sugar*
1 red pepper, diced	*¼ teaspoon garlic*
1 onion, diced	*Cornstarch*
1 cup broccoli	

Bring 4 cups water to boil. Combine rice and water, cook for 20 minutes, put rice aside in separate container. Put in peanut oil, begin adding vegetables when oil is hot. (Vegetables should be added in accordance to recipe list above.) Cook from 2-3 minutes, add bean sprouts last. Cook about 30 seconds. Move vegetables aside and mix sauce. Add cornstarch last, mixing until thickened. Take vegetables out and put rice back in. Make a depression in rice and fill with vegetables and sauce. Serve.

NEW PEAS AND POTATOES

Lynn and Tonia Hopkins, a young couple who were fairly new to Dutch oven cooking, took a 3rd place on Vegetable Day with this delicious vegetable combo.

12" Dutch oven
Serves 15-20

5 lbs. new red potatoes
4 cups fresh or frozen peas
1 cube butter or margarine
1 heaping tablespoon each thyme, rosemary, and tarragon
12 heaping tablespoons flour
8 cups milk
Salt and pepper to taste

Scrub the potatoes. Leaving the skins on, cut into 1 inch pieces. Place in Dutch oven and cover with water. Add 1 tablespoon salt. Boil until tender when pierced with a fork. Add the peas and cook 5 minutes more. Drain and set aside.

Melt butter in Dutch oven. Add spices and sauté for a few minutes. Add flour and mix well (I find a wire whip to be especially nice). Add milk very slowly, stirring vigorously. (If the milk is added too quickly, the sauce will be lumpy.) Stir constantly until the sauce has thickened. Add the potatoes and peas. Serve immediately.

FRENCH FRIES

These are fun to make when barbecuing hamburgers.

Fill your Dutch oven about one-half full of cooking oil and heat until oil is lightly smoking. Add freshly cut or frozen french fries and fry until golden brown.

MIXED VEGGIE DELIGHT

Another nice garden mix from a veteran Dutch oven cook, Bonnie Chambers, from Vegetable Day at the Cookoff.

10 small new red potatoes
10 carrots
½ head cauliflower
2 bunches broccoli
20 baby onions (or green onions)
2 cups mozzarella cheese
1 cup mild cheese
½ cup Parmesan cheese
½ can olives, sliced

Cut vegetables in desired sizes. (The smaller they are, the faster they cook.) Simmer approximately 1½ hours in 12" Dutch oven. Vegetables should still be a little firm.

Before serving, top with mozzarella and mild cheese. Sprinkle olives over cheese. Sprinkle Parmesan cheese over olives. Cover and let stand 5 minutes, then serve.

SUMMER DELIGHT

Mick and Kathie Miller from American Fork, Utah enjoy cooking this fun and easy vegetable recipe.

10" Dutch oven
Serves 6

7 yellow crookneck summer squash, sliced
½ green bell pepper, chopped
½ red bell pepper, chopped
7 green onions, sliced
¼ cup chunky picante sauce, medium hot
½ cup grated mozarella cheese
1 tablespoon butter/margarine

Melt butter in bottom of oven. Layer ingredients in order given. Bake on medium heat 20 minutes. Vegetables will be crisp.

SOUTHERN VEGETABLE CHOW

"Southern Cooking" and Dutch ovens go together according to Gary Bowen and Brian Spring.

12" Dutch oven

4 strips bacon	*1 onion, chopped*
2 cups okra cut into rings	*5 ears corn, kernels scraped*
3 large tomatoes, chopped	*1 green pepper, chopped*
1 teaspoon sugar	*Salt and pepper to taste*
Tabasco to taste	*⅓ cup cilantro, chopped*

In your 12" Dutch oven with 10-12 briquets underneath, cook bacon until crisp. Remove from oven and set aside. Saute' onions and okra in bacon fat. Add corn kernels and sauté another 10 minutes. Add remaining ingredients, except for cilantro. Cover and simmer with coals on top and bottom until done. Stir occasionally. Stir in cilantro and crumble bacon on top. Serve and enjoy.

CHAPTER 6
Breads and Rolls

WHOLE WHEAT AND WHITE DUTCH OVEN DINNER ROLLS

One of Juanita Kohler's favorite foods to make in a Dutch oven is rolls. Here is one of her recipes.

12" Dutch oven

2 cups white flour
1 cup whole wheat flour
1 tablespoon sugar
1 teaspoon salt
1 cup warm milk
1 tablespoon butter

1½ tablespoons yeast
¼ cup warm water
⅛ teaspoon sugar

In a small bowl mix yeast and water, sprinkle ⅛ teaspoon of sugar over the yeast to activate it. In a separate bowl add the flours, 1 tablespoon sugar, salt, warm milk and softened butter. Add yeast to this mixture and knead until smooth. If necessary add small amounts of flour to get the right consistency. Form into a ball and place in a greased bowl to rise. Let rise until double in size. Knead down and let rise a second time. Divide the dough into twelve equal sized rolls. Shape into smooth rolls and place in greased Dutch oven. If you like a crusty, crunchy top to your rolls, press the tops of rolls in whole wheat flour before putting in Dutch oven. Let the rolls rise until about twice their original size. Bake on a bed of medium coals, with coals on top also for approximately 10-15 minutes. Remove Dutch oven from coals and continue cooking from top only for another 10-15 minutes or until rolls are golden brown. Serve piping hot with butter, raspberry freezer jam or honey.

You can "stack" your ovens to save on briquets or coals. It's just a little unhandy when you want to check the one on the bottom.

TRAIL STYLE BAKING POWDER BISCUITS

This is a quick and easy recipe from Dick and Pat Michaud's files that you can whip up just about anywhere. Also try using buttermilk instead of the regular milk.

2 cups white flour
½ teaspoon salt
⅔ cup milk
4 teaspoons baking powder
4 tablespoons lard/shortening

Start with cold ingredients and mix lightly. Sift dry ingredients together. Cut in lard or mix in shortening with fork; slowly add milk. Roll out on floured board to ½ inch to 1 inch thick.

Cut biscuits with cutter or floured glass tumbler. Bake with ⅔ coals on top and ⅓ on bottom to make moderately hot oven for approximately 12-14 minutes. Too hot will make them hard and too slow will make them soggy, so check them a time or two.

ORANGE ROLLS— DUTCH OVEN STYLE

The third dish of the 1st Place winners from Championship Day by Lynn and Sue Packer. They melt in your mouth!

1 cup scalded milk
½ cup sugar
1 cube butter
1 teaspoon salt
½ cup warm water
1 ½ tablespoons yeast
1 teaspoon sugar
5 cups flour
2 eggs

Filling:
1 orange rind, grated
½ cube butter
½ cup sugar

Add milk, sugar, butter, beaten eggs. Mix yeast and 1 teaspoon sugar to ½ cup water. Add to above. Add dry ingredients. Mix well, let rise until double in volume. Roll out jellyroll style and add orange, sugar and butter mixture. Roll up, pinching edges to seal and cut (approximately 1 inch thick) and place in a greased 12" Dutch oven. Let rise until double in volume, then bake for 30-45 minutes (depending on heat of fire). Watch carefully. Cook with coals on top and bottom for first 12-15 minutes, then just on top for remainder of time.

Glaze:
½ cube butter
1 cup powdered sugar
Juice from 1 orange

Pour over top of rolls and sprinkle with sliced almonds. Garnish with orange slices and maraschino cherries.

GOLDEN BUTTERMILK BISCUITS

A Dutch oven cook just can't have too many good biscuit recipes. Here's a smooth buttermilk version from Dick and Pat Michaud.

2 cups all-purpose flour
3 teaspoons baking powder
2 teaspoons sugar
½ teaspoon cream of tartar
¼ teaspoon baking soda
½ cup shortening
¾ cup buttermilk
¼ teaspoon salt

Stir together flour, baking powder, sugar, cream of tartar, soda and salt. Cut in shortening till mixture looks like course crumbs. Fashion a well in the middle. Add milk quickly and stir just till the dough clings together. Knead gently on lightly floured surface for 10-12 strokes. Roll or pat out to ½ inch thick. Cut with floured biscuit cutter or tumbler. Bake in moderately hot oven with ⅔ coals on top and ⅓ on bottom for 10-12 minutes or till golden brown on top. Check progress at about 7-8 minutes. Serve the 10-12 biscuits warm with honey or jam.

ZUCCHINI BREAD

It has been said that one zucchini plant is enough for a whole neighborhood, Wallace and Pat Kohler are trying to disprove this theory.

12" Dutch oven
Serves 15-20

Ingredients:
3 eggs
2 cups sugar
1 cup vegetable oil
3 cups flour
3 teaspoons cinnamon
1 teaspoon salt
1 teaspoon soda
1 teaspoon baking powder
1 teaspoon vanilla
2 cups peeled and grated zucchini
1 cup nuts (optional)

Beat together eggs and sugar. Add vegetable oil and then flour, cinnamon, salt, soda, baking powder and vanilla. Fold in zucchini and nuts.

Pour into a lightly greased Dutch oven and bake with coals on both the top and bottom for 15 minutes. Then bake with coals only on the top for another 45 minutes or until done.

PIZZA DOUGH

Pat Kohler's family really goes for this one.

½ cup warm water
1 tablespoon dry yeast
1 cup flour
½ teaspoon salt
2 tablespoons oil

Add yeast to water and let stand a few minutes. Mix all ingredients and allow dough to rise until doubled in volume. Set container in hot water or in the sun. If you intend to remove the pizza from your Dutch oven for serving, you may wish to line the oven with foil. If you intend to serve the pizza right from the Dutch oven, just grease the bottom of the oven. Put some oil on your fingers and spread the dough over the bottom and slightly up the sides of your Dutch oven. Add pizza sauce, desired toppings and cheese. Bake pizza in a 14″ Dutch oven. Bake with most of the coals on the top for about 20 minutes, checking crust occasionally to make sure it doesn't burn.

BREAD STICKS

This recipe from Wallace and Pat Kohler is fairly fast and is especially popular with children.

16″ Dutch oven
Serves 10-15

Ingredients:

1½ cup warm water   *1 teaspoon salt*
1 tablesppoon yeast   *4 cups flour*
1 tablespoon malted milk powder   *1 cube butter*
1 tablespoon honey   *Parmesan cheese*

Mix together all ingredients, except flour. Stir until well dissolved. Add flour, mix and knead (about 2-3 minutes) until most of the stickiness is gone. Sprinkle on flour as needed. Shape dough like a French loaf and cut into 15 equal pieces. Roll pieces into sticks and place in an ungreased Dutch oven. Spoon over bread dough a cube of melted butter and sprinkle with Parmesan cheese. Let rise at least 20 minutes. Bake with ⅓ of the coals on the bottom and ⅔ of the coals on the lid for 15 minutes or until golden brown.

DUTCH OVEN ROLLS

To watch Juanita Kohler generate these at a workshop is to watch an artist at work.

1 tablespoon yeast
¼ cup warm water
⅛ teaspoon sugar
1 teaspoon salt
1 tablespoon sugar
3 cups flour
1 cup warm milk
1 tablespoon butter

This recipe fits in a 12″ Dutch oven. Approximately 1 dozen rolls.

Mix dry yeast in water, sprinkle the ⅛ teaspoon sugar over the yeast mixture to activate. Mix milk, butter, salt and sugar, stir well. Add one-half amount of flour, mix thoroughly. Add yeast mixture, stir well, then add the rest of the flour (retaining ½ cup). The dough will be stiff. Sprinkle some of the remaining flour on a flat surface. Knead until dough is smooth. Place dough in greased bowl, cover and let rise until double in bulk (approximately 1 hour). Shape dough into smooth rolls and place in greased Dutch oven. Cover and let rise until double in bulk. Place the Dutch oven on one or two shovels of hot coals and also put a shovel of coals on the top of the lid. Bake approximately 10-15 minutes from top and bottom. Remove Dutch oven from coals and continue baking with coals on top for approximately 10-15 minutes or until rolls are golden brown.

Variation:

Orange Rolls:　　*½ square of butter*
　　　　　　　　Rind from 1 orange
　　　　　　　　½ cup sugar

Cinnamon Rolls:　*Brown sugar, cinnamon*
　　　　　　　　raisins or nuts as desired

Roll dough in a flat rectangle shape (approximately ¼ inch thick). Spread or sprinkle the filling on the roll dough. Roll up and pinch edges together. Cut in 1 inch slices and place in greased Dutch oven, edges touching. Let rise until double in bulk. Bake in the same manner as the Dutch oven rolls.

Generally all baking requires more heat on top of the oven than is required on the bottom. Rotate your oven ¼-½ turn once or twice while baking. This regulates the uneven heat caused by wind and/or the uneven distribution of coals on the top and bottom of your oven.

CORN BREAD—SOUTHERN STYLE

Corn bread goes with just about anything.

1 cup all purpose flour
1 cup yellow cornmeal
¼ cup sugar
4 teaspoons baking powder
¾ teaspoon salt
2 eggs
1 cup milk
¼ cup cooking oil or shortening

Mix flour, cornmeal, sugar, baking powder and salt. Add eggs, milk and oil or melted shortening. Beat just until smooth. Pour into a well-oiled 12″ Dutch oven and place on bed of coals; add coals to top of Dutch oven. Bake for 10-15 minutes, remove from coals and continue baking from top only for an additional 10-15 minutes or until bread is golden brown.

SUPER MOIST CORN BREAD

Here's another variation on a favorite food.

2 cups cornmeal
2 cups flour
1 teaspoon salt
7 teaspoons baking powder
2 cups milk
½ cup oil
2 eggs
1 yellow cake mix (the kind with pudding is even better)

Set aside cake mix. Mix all dry ingredients, then mix remaining ingredients in a separate bowl. Combine the two mixtures and set aside. Prepare the yellow cake mix according to package directions. Combine cake mixture with the first mixture. Pour into a well greased 14″ Dutch oven. Bake with coals on top and bottom of your Dutch oven for 12-15 minutes. Bake about 15 minutes more with coals just on top. Use a toothpick to see if bread is done before removing it from the heat.

This cornbread is excellent served with BBQ spareribs.

Before there were briquets, the cowboy cook often had to use "prairie coal" or cow chips. Frank Tolbert in "A Bowl of Red" reports that "There has been more bread burned in Dutch ovens heated by cow chips than by any kind of wood."

NAVAHO FRY BREAD

Here's a fun treat the Michauds and Kohlers think you and your kids will want to make time after time.

2 cups white flour
2 teaspoons baking powder
½ teaspoon salt
½ cup nonfat dry milk
Water (enough to form dough)

Mix all ingredients and knead until the dough is soft and elastic. Let stand for two hours covered with a cloth. Then pinch off pieces about the size of a small egg and roll and pat them between your hands until they are about ¼ inch thick and six inches across. Melt enough lard or shortening in a 14" Dutch oven to make it about one inch deep. Heat to a hot temperature. Poke a small hole in the rounds of dough and fry on one side till brown, then turn and fry other side. Drain on paper towel and serve with honey butter, jam or plain honey.

DILLY BREAD

Dave and Carol Johnson use this excellent specialty bread to compliment any meal.

12" Dutch oven
Serves 8-10 (loaf)
8 (rolls)

Ingredients:

1 yeast cake	*2 teaspoons dill seed*
¼ cup warm water	*1 teaspoon salt*
1 cup cream style cottage cheese	*¼ teaspoon soda*
2 tablespoons sugar	*1 unbeaten egg*
1 tablespoon instant onion	*2½ cups sifted flour*
1 tablespoon butter	

Heat cottage cheese and butter to lukewarm in Dutch oven. A small "cup" of heavy duty tinfoil placed in the oven will work and ease clean-up. Add yeast to warm water and set aside. Add cottage cheese, onion, butter, dill seed, salt and egg in a large bowl and mix well. Add yeast mixture. Sift flour and soda and mix to a soft dough. The dough may be made into rolls or a single loaf. Place in a greased Dutch oven. A 10 inch pie plate may be used in the bottom of the Dutch oven to ensure a non-burning, evenly browned bottom crust. Rest the plate on small pebbles or 6 small clean machine nuts to keep the bottom of the plate and the Dutch oven evenly separated. Let rise until double and bake at medium heat for 40-45 minutes. Use heat on both the top and bottom for about 15 minutes, then continue cooking with top heat until the crust is a golden brown. While hot, brush with butter and sprinkle with salt. Cut after the loaf has cooled a little, serve with butter.

DUTCH OVEN BISQUICKS

From two gals who really know their way around a campfire, Janae Lee and Shelly Bliss, a quick and simple biscuit recipe.

4 cups bisquick mix
1¼ cups milk
2 eggs
2 teaspoons baking powder

Mix all ingredients together. Drop spoonsful of dough in a circle around the outside of a 12″ Dutch oven, then fill in the middle. Cover and bake about 20-25 minutes or until golden brown. Cook with coals on top of lid also.

DUTCH OVEN FRENCH BREAD

Wynn and Cecelie Costly give us a recipe which looks harder than it is, and the results are worth the effort.

2½ cups warm water
2 tablespoons sugar
2 tablespoons oil
1 tablespoon salt
2 tablespoons yeast
6 cups flour
Butter or margarine
1 egg

Warm the water in your Dutch oven, pour into bowl and add sugar and yeast. After yeast has blossomed, add oil, salt, and half of the flour. Beat. Let rest 10 minutes, then knead and rest four more times. (10 minute rests). Form into four loaves that will set side by side in your 12″ or 14″ Dutch oven. Butter bottom and sides. Set in loaves and cover. Let rise until double. Slash with knife, brush tops with beaten egg. Cover and bake, coals on top and bottom, about 30 minutes. Be careful and check often to make sure fire is not too hot.

To warm up breads or rolls in a Dutch oven, put 4 tablespoons of water in the oven, place on a rack and warm for 15 minutes.

QUICK ROLLS

Doyle and Jan Knudsen provide us with a variation on everybody's favorite—rolls.

1 cup warm water
1 package dry yeast
2 tablespoons sugar
2½ cups flour
1 teaspoon salt
1 egg
2 tablespoons vegetable oil

Dissolve yeast in water with sugar. Sift flour and salt together, then mix egg and oil together. Mix egg mixture with yeast and half the flour. Beat with wooden spoon until smooth. Mix in rest of flour until smooth. Knead. Cover and let the dough rise until double in size, about 30 minutes. Punch dough down and knead into smooth balls and place in a greased 12″ Dutch oven.

Slightly grease the top of the rolls with butter. Let rise again about 30 more minutes. Slice through top of dough with a sharp knife to form 2 inch squares. Bake until brown, about 20-25 minutes, with coals on the top and bottom for the first 12 minutes. Then finish baking with coals on top only. Serves 12.

QUICK BREADS

This is a general title given to breads or rolls which are made with baking powder instead of yeast. There are a zillion recipes of this kind, such as banana nut, zucchini, orange nut, carrot, etc. They are all good and are produced easily in a Dutch oven as shown here in Dick Michaud's sample recipe.

3 eggs
1 cup oil
2 cups sugar or
  1½ cups honey
2 cups flour
3 teaspoons vanilla
2 teaspoons baking powder

¼ teaspoon soda
2 teaspoons cinnamon
1 teaspoon ginger
2 cups grated zucchini
  (some folks like to grate
  in skins and all)
1 cup chopped walnuts

Combine the eggs, oil and sugar/honey; and then add the remainder of the ingredients in order. Pour into two greased and floured bread pans which will fit your 14″ oven. Bake in a moderate to hot Dutch oven until they pass the toothpick test. Remember to keep about two times as many briquets or coals on top as on the bottom.

 In baking bread, rolls and cobbler, remember there is only a moment or so between just right and burned.

PAUL'S CINNAMON ROLLS

Dick Michaud stole this recipe from his friend Paul Randle, a river rat and anything else that takes place in the out-of-doors. (He also has tried unsuccessfully on many occasions to steal Paul's latest hot fishing spot.)

DOUGH:
1 quart warmed milk (powdered or canned is fine)
2 packages of dry yeast
¼ cup lukewarm water
2 tablespoons sugar
2 eggs beaten
2 tablespoons oil
1½ teaspoons salt
3 teaspoons baking powder
½ teaspoon baking soda
8 cups flour

FILLING:
Lots of granulated sugar, cinnamon, chopped walnuts, raisins, etc.

Dissolve yeast in warm water, then mix ingredients into a smooth, soft dough. Add sufficient flour to enable you to knead until no longer sticky. Let rise once, then punch down and roll out to about ½ inch thick and 12 inches wide. Sprinkle heavily with sugar, cinnamon, raisins, chopped walnuts and any other goodies you fancy. Press or roll all this good stuff into the dough, then roll up the whole thing, seal the edges and slice into pieces about 1½ inches thick. Coat your hands with oil and shape these slices into rolls about 4 inches in diameter and ¾ inch thick. Place them bumper to bumper in a cold 12″ Dutch oven and then place oven on the coals and heap more coals on the lid. Don't tinker with the lid until about 10-15 minutes after you smell the rolls baking, then check if you must.

After the rolls cool, I like to glaze mine with a tasty glaze made of two cubes of real butter, mashed up with enough powdered sugar to make it good and thick. Then add 1 teaspoon of vanilla and enough canned milk to make it nice and creamy. Put it on thick.

 Clean up, wipe up, discard packaging as you go.

SOFT PRETZELS

Why not Dutch oven pretzels.

1 package dry yeast
1 tablespoon water
1 egg
4 cups flour

1 tablespoon sugar
1 teaspoon salt
1½ cups warm water

Dissolve yeast in 1½ cups of water in a large bowl. Mix flour, salt, sugar in another large bowl. Mix 3 cups of the flour mixture into the yeast and water mixture. Knead until well blended and then add the remaining flour mixture. Shape into pretzels and place in your greased Dutch oven. Coat each pretzel with a mixture of the 1 egg and 1 tablespoon of water. Let rise for 15-20 minutes and then bake with coals on top and bottom for about 12 minutes, remove from the coals and continue baking until golden brown.

CHAPTER 7
Desserts

GREAT GRANDMA KOHLER'S APPLE STRUDEL

Many a Kohler has enjoyed this scrumptious apple dessert from the kitchen of Grandma Rosa. Mike and Juanita Kohler say it is delicious in a Dutch oven too.

1 cup shortening	*1 tablespoon vinegar*
1 teaspoon salt	*¼ cup milk*
2½ cups flour	*1 egg (beat slightly)*

Combine the flour, salt and shortening together. Mix the vinegar and the milk together and add to the flour mixture. Add the beaten egg. Roll out on a floured surface, in a large enough circle to cover the bottom and go up the sides (2 inches) of a 12″ Dutch oven.

Filling:

12 cups thinly sliced, peeled cooking apples (4 pounds)
1 cup sugar
1 teaspoon ground cinnamon
¼ teaspoon salt
3 tablespoons butter
3 eggs
2 tablespoons condensed milk

Fill your pastry lined Dutch oven with the sliced apples. Mix cinnamon, sugar and salt together and sprinkle over apples. Dot with butter. Beat eggs and condensed milk and pour over apples. Bake with coals on top and bottom for approximately 15-20 minutes, then remove Dutch oven from fire and continue baking from top only until golden brown. This will take approximately 15-20 more minutes. Serve with half and half cream, ice cream or all by itself.

APPLE CAKE WITH CARAMEL SAUCE

This Second Place finisher on Championship Day was the "sweet" work of Tyrone Lewis and Larry Lewis.

Cream:
 1 cup shortening
 2 cups sugar
 3 eggs

Combine and add to sugar mixture:
 2 teaspoons vanilla
 4 cups apples, finely chopped
 3 cups flour
 2 teaspoons cinnamon
 1½ teaspoons nutmeg
 ½ cup nuts
 2 teaspoons soda dissolved in
 1 tablespoon boiling water

Sprinkle top with sugar. Bake in a 12″ Dutch oven for 15 minutes with coals on top and bottom. Bake an additional 45 minutes with coals on top only.

Caramel Sauce:
 1 cup brown sugar
 1 cup sugar
 1½ cups heavy cream
 ¾ cup butter
 2 teaspoons vanilla

Cook for 5 minutes and serve warm.

DUTCH OVEN TRIPLE TREAT

Here is a way, by Ron Campbell and Al MacQueen, to have three of your favorite tastes all in one pie. It took Second Place for them.

Place pie crust in your 12″ Dutch oven. Divide into 3 equal sections by making dividers from leftover crust dough. (Use your own favorite crust recipe.) Make sure that the crust is equal height all around oven with the dividers approximately ¼ inch lower than highest crust edge.

Add 3 different fruit fillings, one to each section. Now prepare lattice top by using ½ inch strips of extra dough. Bake with coals on top and bottom until done. Should be served with good homemade ice cream.

FRUIT PIZZA

This recipe of Wallace and Pat Kohler's is quick to make and is a real eye catcher.

14" Dutch oven
Serves 10-15

Ingredients:

Crust	Filling
⅓ cup butter	*8 oz. cream cheese*
½ cup sugar	*½ cup sugar*
1 egg	*1 teaspoon vanilla*
⅛ cup milk	
2 cups flour	*Mix and spread filling on*
1 teaspoon soda	*the crust like frosting.*
⅛ teaspoon salt	
½ teaspoon vanilla	*Top with your favorite fruits.*

Mix the butter and sugar together, add the egg and milk and continue mixing. Add the flour, soda and salt and mix until blended. Add the vanilla. Lightly grease your Dutch oven. Roll out the dough to fit the bottom of your Dutch oven. Bake with a few coals on the bottom and most on the top for 5-10 minutes. Remove the crust from the Dutch oven as you would a pineapple upside-down cake.

Arrange your favorite fruit on the cream cheese layer in rows, circles or in whatever design you like. Any combination of fruit may be used. For example: sliced kiwi, orange pieces, apple and banana slices, grapes, strawberries or other kinds of berries or use pie filling.

Sprinkle fresh fruit with Fruit Fresh or make a glaze by combining 1 cup orange juice, ½ cup sugar and 2 tablespoons cornstarch. Cook these ingredients, cool and pour over fruit.

SPICY WALNUT-RAISIN PIE

Someone accused Brent Checketts and Richard Heiner of winning First Place with the six-guns they wore. But after you whip this one up, you'll know it was the recipe. Or was it the rum in the sauce?

Pastry for 9-inch single-crust pie

2 eggs
½ cup sugar
¼ teaspoon salt
¼ teaspoon each—ground cinnamon, nutmeg, and cloves
¾ cup corn syrup
¼ cup butter, melted
⅓ cup chopped walnuts, coarse
⅓ cup raisins

Prepare pastry. Beat eggs, sugar, salt, cinnamon, nutmeg, cloves, corn syrup and butter. Stir in walnuts and raisins. Pour into pastry-lined pie plate. Bake in 12" Dutch oven with space under pie (inverted pie pan) until filling is set, 40-50 minutes. Serve warm or cool with sauce.

Butterscotch-Rum Sauce:

⅔ cup sugar
⅓ cup butter
⅓ cup buttermilk
2 teaspoons corn syrup
¼ teaspoon baking soda
1 tablespoon rum or 1 teaspoon rum flavoring

In your Dutch oven heat sugar, butter, buttermilk, corn syrup and baking soda. Heat to boiling over medium coals, stirring constantly. Boil 5 minutes, stirring frequently. Remove from coals, stir in rum, cool completely.

DUTCH OVEN FRUIT COCKTAIL PUDDING CAKE

Marcia Craw Moss and Kathy Hogan won Third Place on Bread and Dessert Day with a fruit cocktail takeoff on the pineapple upside down idea.

Grease, not oil, your 12" Dutch oven just before using . Pour into Dutch oven 6 cups of fruit plus juice.

I use:
2 1-lb cans of fruit cocktail packed in juice
1 1-lb can of chunk pineapple packed in juice

Mix together:
3 cups flour
3 teaspoons soda
1½ teaspoons salt
2 cups sugar
3 slightly beaten eggs
½-1 cup water (Use more water for a lighter cake)

Pour on top of fruit cocktail in Dutch oven.

Sprinkle the batter with 1½ cups brown sugar and 1½ cups nuts, chopped.

Bake with coals on top and bottom. If using briquets, I use approximately 10 underneath and 15 on top. Check occasionally—bake for about 35-40 minutes. You can serve it in the oven or turn out onto a platter for an upside down look. Really pretty. Serve alone or with a scoop of whipping cream.

APRICOT ALMONDINE PIE

Are these ladies, Peggy Roskelley and Rosemary Parkinson, into pies? We'd say so! This one was their Dessert Third Place winner on Championship Day.

Makes a 10" Dutch oven pie
Prepare pastry using 2½ cups flour

6 cups fresh apricots, pitted
1½ cups sugar
3 tablespoons flour
½ teaspoon nutmeg
½ teaspoon almond extract
½ cup slivered almonds (or as desired)
¼ cup butter
Dash of salt

Mix sugar, flour, nutmeg and salt. Mix with fresh apricots. Add almond extract and almonds. Heap into pie shell and dot with butter. Place top crust. Crimp edges. Bake in Dutch oven with coals on bottom and top. Bake until golden brown.

PEACHY SPICE UPSIDE-DOWN CAKE

This peach creation by Shayne, son of Mike and Juanita Kohler, is a sure bet for pleasing any incurable sweet tooth.

2 cups all-purpose flour
1 teaspoon salt
¾ teaspoon baking soda
¾ teaspoon ground cinnamon
1 cup buttermilk or sour milk
¾ cup packed brown sugar

1 cup granulated sugar
1 teaspoon baking powder
¾ teaspoon ground cloves
⅔ cup shortening
3 eggs

4 tablespoons butter
½ cup brown sugar
4-5 peaches
8-10 cherries

In a mixing bowl combine the flour, granulated sugar, salt, baking powder, baking soda, cloves and cinnamon. Add shortening, ¾ cup brown sugar and buttermilk or sour milk; mix until all the flour is moistened, approximately 4 minutes. Add eggs and continue to mix for approximately 2 more minutes.

In the bottom of a 12″ Dutch oven melt 4 tablespoons of butter and ½ cup brown sugar. Slice thin, 4-5 fresh peaches and arrange in the Dutch oven, garnish with maraschino cherries (cut in half, round side down). Pour the cake mix over the peaches. Place coals on the top and bottom of the Dutch oven and bake over medium coals for approximately 14 minutes. Remove Dutch oven from coals and continue baking from top only until golden brown. Test with toothpick for doneness. Remove coals from top and let set for 2-3 minutes, then invert on a tinfoil covered cardboard round. Garnish with mint leaf and whipped cream.

DUTCH OVEN APPLE PIE

One of the most absolutely gorgeous sights you'll ever see is one of Paul Randle's lattice-covered apple pies in a Dutch oven. He says that he dreamed up the recipe on the Middle Fork of the Salmon River years ago and it has never failed him since.

Use a 14″ oven and a 12 inch pie pan.

Make enough pie crust for a two-crust pie (use pie crust sticks) and put the bottom crust in the pie tin. Slice into this enough sour cooking apples to fill it to the top of the tin. Pour over the apples a custard mixture made of three beaten eggs, ¼ cup condensed milk, lots of cinnamon (it's hard to get too much) and enough granulated sugar to make the goop the consistency of Prell Shampoo. The custard rises (and is like shellac in a cold Dutch oven) so don't fill the pie tin more than ¼-⅓ full. Put a lattice crust on the top, sprinkle with granulated sugar and bake until golden brown. Expect whistles of admiration when you whip the lid off the finished creation.

Fresh (not cooked) rhubarb and sour cherries also work really well in this recipe.

RAISIN TURNOVERS

For an old fashioned treat, try Anne Godfrey and Phyllis Richards raisin turnovers.

14" Dutch oven
Serves 30

Ingredients:
½ cup shortening
1 egg
1 cup sugar
½ cup milk
1 teaspoon vanilla
3 cups flour
1 teaspoon baking powder
1 teaspoon soda
1 teaspoon salt

Filling:
1 cup raisins (ground)
½ cup water
1 tablespoon flour
½ cup sugar
½ cup nuts (ground)

Cream together shortening, egg, and sugar, then add milk and vanilla; mix. Add flour, baking powder, soda and salt and mix well. Chill dough and roll out on floured board.

Filling: Boil together raisins and water, then mix flour and sugar together and add to boiling raisins. Add ground nuts to raisin mixture. Cut dough into squares big enough for 2 teaspoons of filling, fold over and press edges together. Place on a small greased cookie sheet or pizza pan or directly in the Dutch oven and bake for 10 minutes. (Put 7 briquets on the bottom and 14 briquets on the top.)

PINEAPPLE UPSIDE-DOWN CAKE

Dick Michaud remembers foundering on this delicacy cooked by an old cowboy up on the headwaters of the Green River in Wyoming. Here's the Kohler recipe.

½ cup brown sugar
¼ cup butter
Maraschino cherries

1 can sliced pineapple
1 yellow cake mix
3 eggs

Put butter and brown sugar in a 14" Dutch oven and melt while stirring over warm fire. Place the pineapple slices in the butter and sugar mixture and place halved maraschino cherries in each pineapple center. In a separate container prepare the cake mix according to the instructions on the package. Pour batter over pineapple and place lid on the Dutch oven. Place oven on a medium hot bed of coals, making sure your Dutch oven is kept level, add a shovelful of coals on top of oven; cook for approximately 15 minutes. Remove oven from coals, continue cooking with coals on top only approximately 15-20 minutes or until golden brown. Make sure your cake is completely baked by inserting a toothpick into cake. If toothpick comes out clean, your cake is done. Cool for about 10 minutes, remove from oven and serve. A helpful hint for removing cake from Dutch oven is to use a round piece of cardboard covered with aluminum foil; cut to fit inside your Dutch oven. Set the cardboard round on cake and invert Dutch oven.

HUCKLEBERRY PIE

Whatever your taste in berries is, this will work with it. But don't forget to try it with the huckleberries sometime, or you'll be missing one of life's great treats according to Mike Kohler.

Crust:

2½ cups flour	*1 tablespoon vinegar*
1 teaspoon salt	*¼ cup milk*
1 cup shortening	*1 egg (whipped)*

Mix the flour, salt and shortening together; add vinegar to the milk and combine with the flour mixture. Add one egg. Divide in half and roll out on a floured surface. Place in a 7½ inch pie pan. Put in huckleberry filling, or your favorite filling. Roll out second half of dough making slits in the dough to allow for steam. Place on top and seal edges with milk, then flute edges.

Filling:

1 quart berries	*2 teaspoons vanilla*
2 cups water	*2 tablespoons butter*
½ cup sugar	*2-3 tablespoons cornstarch*

Start with 1 quart berries and 1½ cups water. Bring this to a boil and add ½ cup sugar. Mix ½ cup water and 2-3 tablespoons of cornstarch. Mix well. Pour into boiling fruit mixture until thickened. Add a dash of salt, 2 teaspoons vanilla and 2 tablespoons of butter. Pour into prepared pie shell. Bake in a 10″ Dutch oven on a wire rack or an inverted pie pan. Bake with coals on top and bottom for approximately 15-20 minutes, then remove from fire and continue baking from top only until golden brown, approximately 15-20 minutes longer. (This pie can also be baked directly in the Dutch oven.)

 A round cake rack or grill, placed in the bottom of the oven, keeps vegetables from getting boiled instead of steamed and helps keep pie and bread tins (if you use them) off the hot bottom. Put three pennies or pebbles underneath your tins to let the air circulate underneath and prevent hot spots.

LEMON CAKE DESSERT

Wallace and Pat Kohler claim this cake should be called wonder cake because it will disappear so fast you will wonder where it went.

12" Dutch oven
Serves 12-15

Ingredients:
1 regular yellow cake mix
1 3 oz. package lemon jello
¾ cup salad oil
¾ cup water
4 eggs

Icing:
2 cups powdered sugar
juice of 2 lemons or
4-5 tablespoons bottled
lemon juice

Lightly grease and flour your Dutch oven. Mix dry Jello with cake mix, add the other ingredients and beat into a batter. Pour the batter into the Dutch oven and bake with coals on top and bottom for 15 minutes. Finish baking with coals just on the lid about 15 more minutes. When done, wait 5 minutes, then prick all over the top of the cake with a fork and pour icing over cake.

Whipped cream or Cool Whip may be added as topping, if desired, when the cake is cool.

MEXICAN OATMEAL CAKE

Joseph and Wendy Rodriguez give us a fine and different cake from their national heritage.

Combine:
1 cup oatmeal (regular)
1½ cups boiling water

Add:
1 cup brown sugar
1 cup sugar
2 eggs
½ cup oil

Let stand until cool.

Sift in:
1½ cups flour
1 teaspoon soda
1 teaspoon salt
1 teaspoon cinnamon

Pour batter into foil-lined 12" Dutch oven. Cook 10-20 minutes with minimal heat on bottom and majority on top.

Frosting:
6 tablespoons butter
¾ cup brown sugar
¼ cup canned milk

Boil together for 5 minutes. Add ½ cup pecans. Spread over cake while warm.

DUTCH OVEN GERMAN CHOCOLATE CHEESECAKE

Here's one to satisfy both your urge to whip up something different and good at the same time. It's by Wynn and Cecelie Costley.

Crust:

2 cups crushed Oreos
1 cube melted margarine
1 tablespoon sugar

Melt butter in warm Dutch oven then pour over Oreos in bowl; add sugar and mix well, then press into 9 inch glass or aluminum pie plate. Chill while making filling.

Filling:

¼ cup sugar
3 eggs
1½ package (8 oz.) cream cheese, softened
8 oz. milk chocolate chips, melted
1 cup sour cream
2 tablespoons cocoa
1 teaspoon vanilla
¼ cup margarine

In your Dutch oven, combine chocolate chips, cocoa and margarine, melt. In a bowl, beat the eggs and sugar until fluffy; add cream cheese and beat until smooth. Blend in sour cream and vanilla and finally fold in melted chocolate and margarine. Pour into crust. Wipe out Dutch oven and arrange 3 tinfoil lumps in Dutch oven to keep pie plate up off the bottom. Bake with slow coals on bottom and lid of oven for about 45 minutes. Cool completely.

Frosting:

⅔ cup brown sugar
⅓ cup margarine
¼ cup light cream
1⅓ cups shredded or flaked coconut
½ teaspoon vanilla
½ cup chopped walnuts

While pie cools, melt margarine in oven. Add coconut and brown. Remove from oven and add brown sugar, light cream and vanilla. Beat well, add nuts and spread over cheesecake. Top with a cherry and finish cooking.

"I long for a whiff of bacon and beans, a snug shakedown in the snow;
A trail to break, and a life at stake, and another bout with the foe."
Robert W. Service, *The Heart of the Sourdough*

CHOCOLATE MAYONNAISE CAKE WITH RASPBERRY SAUCE

You haven't lived with a Dutch oven until you've tried a cake. Here's a good sample from Marcia Craw Moss, Kathy Hogan and Jane Gyllenskog.

1 cup sugar
2 cups flour
2 teaspoons soda
2 tablespoons cocoa
¼ teaspoon salt

1 cup mayonnaise
1 cup water
1 teaspoon vanilla

Sift together all dry ingredients, then add 1 cup mayonnaise, 1 cup water and 1 teaspoon vanilla. Beat until well-blended. Bake 45 minutes to 1 hour in Dutch oven with coals on top and bottom for first 15 minutes, then just from top for the remainder of the time. Looks nice in a bundt pan.

Sauce:
Use 1 package raspberry Danish Dessert, add 1½ cups water. Bring to a boil, stirring constantly, boil for 1 minute. Add 2 cups fresh or frozen raspberries and 1 teaspoon vanilla.

APPLE CRISP

Another very popular recipe. This one from Doyle and Jan Knudsen and the World Championship Dutch Oven Cookoff.

Filling:
2 cans apple pie filling
½ cup chopped nuts

Topping Mixture:
1½ cups flour
½ cup rolled oats
¼ teaspoon salt
½ teapoon soda
½ cup brown sugar
½ cup white sugar
12 tablespoons butter

Pour 2 cans of apple pie filling into a 12″ Dutch oven. In a separate container, cut 12 tablespoons butter into dry ingredients of topping mixture and sprinkle on top of apple pie filling, then sprinkle on the nuts. Cook approximately 1 hour with most of the coals on top of the Dutch oven and a smaller amount on the bottom. Check often.

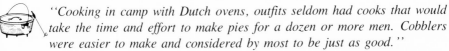

"Cooking in camp with Dutch ovens, outfits seldom had cooks that would take the time and effort to make pies for a dozen or more men. Cobblers were easier to make and considered by most to be just as good."
Stella Hughes in *Chuck Wagon Cookin'*

FRUIT COBBLERS

As indicated in the "starting out" section, the cobbler is an old favorite. We would guess that more folks try this dish as their first attempt at Dutch oven cooking than any other recipe. Cobbler, in our memory, was never made in big enough batches for a troop of Boy Scouts, no matter how Bill Sherwood and Dick Michaud bungled the recipe or the cooking. Thank goodness they have learned how to do it since.

What follows is Dick Michaud's short course in how to "whump" up any kind of fruit cobbler you might imagine, such as apple, cherry, black raspberry, red raspberry, peach, pineapple, strawberry, blueberry, apricot, etc., etc.

1. You can use fresh, canned, bottled, or frozen fruit.
2. When fresh is used, add 1 cup of simple syrup (1 part water to 2 parts sugar).
3. If there is a lot of juice involved, as with bottled peaches, add a couple of heaping tablespoons of tapioca to firm it up.
4. The batter for the top can be a white or yellow cake mix, a golden pound cake mix, or the Bisquick recipe for cobblers. The latter gives a heavier, and some say tastier, result. Some cooks substitute about ¼ cup of water for the egg in the cake mixes.
5. If using frozen fruit, be sure to thaw completely before mixing.
6. Use a healthy sprinkling of cinnamon on the apples before pouring on the batter.
7. (OPTIONAL: Line Dutch oven with aluminum foil to speed up the cleanup.) On smaller ovens, don't have any seams in the foil. On the bigger ovens, triple fold the foil at the seam. Either fold the top edge of the foil down below the pot rim, or trim it accordingly so that the foil will not interfere with the seal of the lid and the pot.
8. A 14″ oven will handle 4 cans, or 3 bottles, or 9 cups of fresh, or 7 10-ounce packages of frozen fruit.
9. Mixing order: in bowl #1, mix fruit, simple syrup (if used), and tapioca (if used). In bowl #2, mix the batter recipe until smooth but still able to pour.
10. Cooking steps:
    - (Optional — line Dutch oven with foil)
    - mix fruit and stuff
    - mix batter
    - level oven on moderate coals
    - put fruit mix in and spread evenly and heat to bubbling
    - pour batter on top and quickly smooth
    - cover with lid and put lots of coals on the lid
    - cobbler should be done in about 30-35 minutes, but you can tell when it's ready because the top will brown and crack. Take oven off bottom coals after 20 minutes.
11. Serve with ice cream or sweetened whipped cream and stand back and wait for the compliments.

 Get all of the members of your family to help with some task. That's where the fun is in preparing meals.

—66—

DUTCH OVEN BAKED APPLES

This is really an easy dessert to prepare but it doesn't last long.

Wash and core apples. Varieties that store well are the best. If you wish, you can fill the apples with extra treats like raisins, sugar, and a little butter. Spices can also be added. Place the apples on a wire rack or in a pie tin that has been raised off the bottom of the Dutch oven a little. Add ¼ inch water and steam with coals both on top and bottom for 20-30 minutes.

CARAMEL NUT UPSIDE-DOWN CAKE

Another variety of a good theme.

¾ cup brown sugar
¼ cup butter
1 cup halved pecans or walnuts

1 yellow cake mix
Eggs for cake mix
Shredded rind from 1 orange

Melt brown sugar and butter in bottom of a 14 " Dutch oven. Place the pecans or walnuts and the shredded orange rind in the brown sugar mixture. In a separate container, prepare the cake mix according to the instructions on the package. Pour the batter over the brown sugar and nut mixture. Place oven on a medium-hot bed of coals. Add a shovelful of coals to top of oven and cook for approximately 15 minutes. Remove oven from coals and continue cooking with coals on top for approximately 15-20 minutes or until golden brown. (Refer to Pineapple Upside-Down Cake for helpful hints on doneness and removal of cake from Dutch oven.)

DUTCH OVEN CARAMEL NUT PUDDING

This is a fantastic Dutch oven dessert

1 tablespoon butter
½ cup milk
½ teaspoon nutmeg
½ cup nuts
½ teaspoon soda

½ cup sugar
1 cup sifted flour
Pinch of salt
1 cup date bits or raisins
1 teaspoon vanilla

Sauce:
1 cup brown sugar
2 tablespoons butter
2 cups boiling water

Cream together the butter and white sugar. Add milk, flour, soda, nutmeg and salt. Mix into a smooth batter. Add the date bits or raisins and nuts. Pour into a greased 10″ Dutch oven. Combine the brown sugar, butter and boiling water for sauce and pour over top of the batter. (Do not stir) Bake with coals on top and bottom for 10-15 minutes. Remove from coals and continue baking until done. Approximately 10-15 minutes more. Good served with ice cream or whipped cream.

CHAPTER 8
Sourdough

JUST A LITTLE HISTORY

Today, we have the name "sourdough" for a type of leavening which has really been around for thousands of years. In the Bible, they talk about "unleavened" bread. Their version of leavened bread was probably the same as our sourdough in that it uses wild yeast spores to generate the carbon dioxide gas to make the bread rise. The miners of Alaska and the Northwest Territories became so identified with the sourdough start that they are generically called "sourdoughs." Pioneer women noted in their diaries that they made "light" bread on the days the wagon train stopped for a day or so. Cowboy cooks were sometimes retained or fired by the quality of their sourdough baking skills.

The "start" is the key to the operation and has often been parked behind the stove to keep it perkin' or wrapped in several bedrolls or even taken to bed during a cold Alaskan winter to keep it healthy. Today, sourdough and Dutch ovens just seem to naturally and nostalgically go together. So try it and gain an enviable skill with your black pots.

SOME GENERAL GROUND RULES FOR THE USE OF SOURDOUGH

1. Starts can be borrowed (the Michauds have one which is reputed to be over 80 years old), bought or made. If you want to "start" one from scratch, here is a simple method. Put a package of dry yeast, one cup of milk, one cup of hard wheat flour in a large non-metal container and let it stand on the cupboard for 2-3 days. By that time it should be bubbling and sending out a pleasant sour aroma which means that you are in business.

2. Don't keep any metal in prolonged contact with the start. The acid in the start reacts with it. Use glass, plastic, or a crock to keep it in.

3. Use daily if you keep it out, about weekly if you keep it in the fridge or every three to five months if you freeze it. When it has been in cold storage, just put it out on the cupboard and in a few hours it will thaw out and start to perk. Also don't put a tight cap on it, the CO_2 will blow the cap and the sourdough all over your habitation.

SOME GENERAL GROUND RULES FOR THE USE OF SOURDOUGH (Continued)

4. If some liquid separates on top, stir it back in if it's orange colored. Throw the whole thing out and start over if it's green colored.

5. Every time you use some of the start, put back in an equal quantity of flour and milk for the amount you want to keep on hand. You can use water but pancakes and rolls will be a little tougher.

6. If your start gets a bit too strong or a bit laid back, take half of it out and replenish with equal amounts of milk and flour and let it stand and revitalize itself.

SOURDOUGH BRAIDED BREAD

Errol and Le Nielson, seasoned Dutch oven cooks from Boise, Idaho, make bread baking seem easy.

16" Dutch oven

Ingredients:
1 cup sourdough
1 cup warm water
1 package dry yeast
3-4 cups flour
½ teaspoon salt
2 teaspoons sugar

Dissolve yeast in warm (not hot) water. Add salt and sugar, mixing thoroughly. Add sourdough and mix well. Stir in flour until dough reaches a consistency to be kneaded by hand. Knead for about 10 minutes until dough is smooth and glossy. Place in mixing bowl, cover and allow to rise until double in size (about 30-40 minutes), punch down. Divide into three equal parts. Roll each out into a rope-like shape about 1 inch in diameter. Braid the three strands together on a cookie sheet lightly sprinkled with cornmeal. Allow to rise until about double in size (20-45 minutes). Then place cookie sheet on three Mason jar rings to hold off bottom of oven and bake 30-60 minutes, or until loaf is brown and sounds hollow when *thumped* with a finger.

Use about 12-15 briquets on bottom and top, adding a few to the top the last 15 minutes of baking, if necessary, to brown the top of the loaf.

NOTE: Sesame seeds can be sprinkled on the loaf just before baking if desired. Also a fine mist of water can be sprayed over the crust two or three times while baking if you desire a *crisper* crust.

"The starter was the basis of practically every meal. From it one could manufacture not only bread, biscuits and flapjacks, but feed the dogs, apply to burns and wounds, chink the log cabin, brew hootch, and, some say, even resole boots."

Don Holm in the *Complete Sourdough Cookbook*

PANCAKES

This is one of Dean Tucker's recipes. His book "Sourdough Cookin" is an expert's collection of recipes and he gladly shares his experiences with interested beginners.

We recommend that you try these first. Cook the pancakes until all the bubbles break and they are dry around the edges.

2 cups start
1 egg
¼ cup evaporated milk
½ teaspoon salt
½ teaspoon soda
2 tablespoons sugar

Mix together start, egg and evaporated milk. Combine the remaining ingredients and sprinkle over the top. Fold in with a large spoon. This may make the batter foam so that the pancakes are nothing but bubbles. If so, wait till it calms down for five minutes or so and then stir it some. Make pancakes about 4 inches in diameter so they will cook through. Use your oven lid upside down on a couple of bricks or rocks as your griddle. Heat lid hot enough to make waterdrops dance.

DUTCH OVEN SOURDOUGH ROLLS

1½ cups warm water
1 package dry yeast (1 tablespoon)
4 cups unsifted flour
2 teaspoons salt
1-2 cups more unsifted flour

1 cup sourdough start
2 teaspoons sugar
½ teaspoon baking soda

Add warm water and yeast. Add sourdough start, 4 cups flour and sugar. Blend well. Cover and place in a warm place (until double in volume, about 2 hours). Mix soda, salt and 1 cup flour. Stir well and add to other mixture. Turn out on a floured board and knead until smooth. Shape in rolls, place in a greased 12″ Dutch oven. When double in bulk, bake from top and bottom on a medium fire for approximately 10-15 minutes. Remove Dutch oven from coals and continue cooking with coals on top for an additional 15-20 minutes or until golden brown.

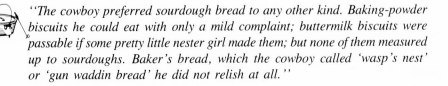

"The cowboy preferred sourdough bread to any other kind. Baking-powder biscuits he could eat with only a mild complaint; buttermilk biscuits were passable if some pretty little nester girl made them; but none of them measured up to sourdoughs. Baker's bread, which the cowboy called 'wasp's nest' or 'gun waddin bread' he did not relish at all."

ALL-AT-ONCE SOURDOUGH BISCUITS

Another Dean Tucker standard.

2 cups flour
2 teaspoons baking powder
¼ teaspoon soda
½ teaspoon salt
3 teaspoons sugar
¼ cup melted shortening
1 cup sourdough start
2 eggs, beaten

Combine the dry ingredients in a bowl, mixing well. Then make a hole in the center and pour in the shortening, sourdough starter and eggs. Mix or knead in the bowl for several minutes. Roll out to ½ inch thickness on a floured breadboard or pinch off golfball sized pieces and shape into biscuits. Use a cutter of some sort if you roll the dough out. Dip both sides of the biscuit in salad oil, melted butter or bacon grease. Place them close together around the outside of your Dutch oven and then fill in the middle as needed. Bake at a moderately hot temperature for 15-20 minutes; again, lots more heat on the top than bottom and check and rotate your oven occasionally. You can improve on these by letting the dough rise for an hour or so before you form the biscuits or after you have placed them in the Dutch oven. You can also use this batter for scones. Just stretch out small pieces and fry in an inch or two of fat. Turn when brown, drain on a paper towel and serve with butter and honey.

"For frontier families, sourdough was the most important possession after the Bible."

Sandra Day, *Country Home*, February, 1986

COTTAGE CHEESE SOURDOUGH BREAD

Rosemary Parkinson and Peggy Roskelley are expert cooks in the kitchen and in the outdoors. They proved their expertise by taking First Place with this tasty sourdough recipe.

14" Dutch oven
1 large loaf (Serves 12)

1 tablespoon dry yeast
2 cups lukewarm water
¾ cup sourdough starter
1 cup creamed cottage cheese
½ cup grated sharp or longhorn cheese
1 tablespoon fresh chopped dill
2 tablespoons fresh chopped onion
1 tablespoon cooking oil or melted shortening
1 tablespoon sugar
1 tablespoon salt
3-4 cups all-purpose flour

Dissolve yeast in lukewarm water. Measure sourdough starter into a large mixing bowl. Add cheese, dill, onion, oil, sugar and salt to starter. Add dissolved yeast. Gradually beat in flour ½ cup at a time, stirring well. Reserve ½ cup flour to work into dough during kneading. Dough should be fairly stiff. Turn out onto lightly floured surface and knead for 5-10 minutes, adding reserved flour if necessary. Put in a greased bowl, turning once. Cover with a cloth. Set in warm place free from drafts and let rise for 2 hours or until doubled in size. Punch dough down. Shape into 3 ropes and braid; cover with a cloth. Set in warm place and let rise for 2 hours or until doubled in size. This rises really fast on a warm day. It is wise to have the coals almost ready when the bread is ready to rise.

Bake in 14" Dutch oven with about 12 coals on the bottom and 18 on top for about 35 minutes.

DUTCH OVEN SOURDOUGH CHOCOLATE CAKE

Sourdough is excellent in desserts. Try this chocolate cake.

⅔ cup shortening
1⅔ cups sugar
3 eggs
1 cup sourdough start
2 cups flour
⅔ cup cocoa

⅔ teaspoon baking powder
1½ teaspoons soda
1 teaspoon salt
¾ cup water
1 teaspoon vanilla
1 cup chopped walnuts (optional,

Cream shortening and sugar. Add eggs one at a time beating after each addition. Stir in start. Mix together flour, cocoa, baking powder, soda and salt. Add alternately with water and vanilla. Grease and lightly flour a 12″ Dutch oven. Pour the batter evenly into the Dutch oven. Bake with coals on top and bottom for 10-15 minutes, remove from coals and continue baking from top only for an additional 10-15 minutes or until cake is done. Allow to cool for ten minutes, then invert on a cardboard round, tinfoil covered. Cool thoroughly and frost with your favorite frosting.

Frosting

6 oz. cream cheese
4 tablespoons butter

½ teaspoon vanilla
1 cup powdered sugar

Blend together until smooth.

CHAPTER 9
Miscellaneous Recipes

ALL-IN-ONE DUTCH OVEN BREAKFAST

If you don't mind eating all of your breakfast items together, Mike and Juanita Kohler think you will love this "All-in-One Dutch Oven Breakfast."

1 lb. breakfast meat	*6-8 eggs*
6-8 potatoes	*½ cube butter*
2 onions	*Seasonings to taste*

Use a 10″ Dutch oven. Fry your favorite breakfast meat; bacon, link sausage, ham, etc. Remove meat when completely cooked, set aside; drain excess oil from Dutch oven. Put sliced potatoes and onions in the Dutch oven along with salt, pepper and other seasonings desired. Add 3-4 pats of butter to top of potatoes and add a small amount of water. Cook until tender from the bottom only. About 20-30 minutes. Remove from fire, cut meat into medium size pieces, place on top of potatoes. Top with 6-8 beaten raw eggs. Replace lid and put coals on top and continue cooking until eggs are done. If you prefer whole eggs, just break 6-8 eggs evenly over the meat and cook from the top until eggs are done to your liking. Serves 6-8 people.

ANYTIME OMELET

This is good anytime you're hungry anytime of the day; not just for breakfast according to Wallace and Pat Kohler.

Use an 8 or 10″ Dutch oven.

Warm the Dutch oven on a bed of coals (low temperature). Add a pat of butter or margarine. Beat 3 eggs and add salt and pepper to taste. Pour into your Dutch oven and cover it. When the eggs are almost cooked, add chopped green onions and tomatoes, sliced mushrooms, cooked bacon, sausage or ham and grated cheese. Fold in half, cover and cook until the cheese melts. Serve over a bed of crisp lettuce.

EASY BAKED BEANS

1 quart can pork 'n beans	*½ teaspoon dry mustard*
½ medium onion, chopped	*⅛ cup ketchup*
¼ cup brown sugar	*Smoked meat*

Brown meat (if necessary) in a 10″ Dutch oven and drain. Remove about one-half of the liquid from the beans and discard. Mix all ingredients and simmer for at least one hour.

LAZY QUICHE

We told you that anything could be cooked in a Dutch oven. Here's the proof.

8 slices white bread	*2 cups milk*
1½ lbs. ground sausage	*1 teaspoon dry mustard*
2 cups grated cheddar cheese	*1 teaspoon salt*
2 green onions, chopped	*Pepper to taste*
8 eggs	*1 can cream of mushroom*
	soup

Remove the crusts from the bread and arrange the slices in the bottom of a 12″ Dutch oven. Add a layer of sausage that has been browned and drained. Add a layer of grated cheese and sprinkle on the green onions. Mix the egg with 1½ cups milk and add the dry mustard, salt and pepper. Pour this mixture over the layers in the Dutch oven. Dilute 1 can cream of mushroom soup with ½ cup milk and pour this over the top of the whole thing. Bake with coals on top and bottom for about 10-15 minutes, then finish with the coals just on the top of the Dutch oven. When it is finished cooking, you can add parsley flakes or chives on top if you wish.

TRAIL BEANS

Deloy and Ron Gardner, a father and son team at the Cookoff, had a number of good, hardy recipes. This is one of them.

1 large can pork and beans
½ cup ketchup
½ cup brown sugar
2 teaspoons dry mustard
4 slices bacon, cut in small pieces
¼ cup molasses
½ green pepper, cut in small pieces
1 medium onion, cut in small pieces

Mix together the above ingredients and put in a 12″ Dutch oven. Cover and simmer over low fire for 2 hours.

DUTCH OVEN LASAGNA

This recipe is simple. It can feed a bunch, can be prepared ahead of time, be put together and cooked when you want. You can double the recipe as many times as you want, just keep adding layers in your Dutch oven(s).

1 ¼ lbs hamburger
6 tablespoons chopped onions
1-10¾-ounce can tomato puree
1 tablespoon Worcestershire sauce
2½ cups water
1 6-ounce can tomato paste

1 tablespoon salt
¼ teaspoon garlic powder
⅛ teaspoon pepper
Lasagna noodles (don't cook)
1 teaspoon sugar
¾ lb. sharp cheese, grated

Brown hamburger and onions in your Dutch oven. Season with salt and pepper, drain. In a separate container blend meat, cheese, sauce, puree, paste, water, sugar and seasonings. Pour some of the sauce in a greased 14″ Dutch oven. Cover with a layer of uncooked lasagna noodles. Repeat layers of sauce and noodles ending with a layer of sauce. Cover and bake with coals on both top and bottom for about one hour.

The sauce is even better if you prepare it ahead of time and refrigerate overnight. YUM!

MIKE'S VEGETABLE OMELET

This breakfast recipe idea came about from an overnight family reunion Mike and Juanita Kohler went to in Dammeron Valley, Utah by Baker Reservoir.

12 eggs
¼ cup milk
1 cup diced ham/bacon or sausage
1 medium onion diced
1 cup sliced mushrooms

1½ cups broccoli
2 cups grated American
*   processed cheese*
Salt and pepper
2 tablespoons butter

In a 10″ Dutch oven cook the meat thoroughly, drain and set aside. Wipe out Dutch oven and steam the onion, broccoli and mushrooms over medium coals for approximately 10 minutes or until onion becomes transparent. Remove vegetables from Dutch oven and set aside. Dry out your Dutch oven with a paper towel; with an oiled paper towel rub sides and bottom of Dutch oven.

In a separate container beat the eggs; add milk, salt, pepper and butter. Fold meat, vegetables and cheese into the beaten eggs.

Pour mixture into your Dutch oven and bake from top and bottom with medium hot coals for approximately 15 minutes. Remove Dutch oven from coals and continue baking from top only for approximately 20 more minutes or until eggs are completely done. Garnish with sliced tomato halves, fresh parsley and parsley flakes. Cut in pie shaped pieces and serve. Excellent all-in-one breakfast or anytime of the day. Serves 6-8 people.

 A handy storage bag for a Dutch oven is a clean (at least to start) burlap bag. Its open weave construction allows for air circulation and padding.

NEW ENGLAND CLAM CHOWDER

This savory clam chowder was a winning recipe prepared by Neil and Carrie Dabb. It was truly a scrumptious New England treat.

10" Dutch Oven
Serves 6-8

2 6½-ounce cans minced clams
1 cup celery, diced
¾ cup butter
1 quart light cream
1½ teaspoons sugar
½ teaspoon very finely chopped fresh parsley
2 cups potatoes, finely diced
1 cup onion finely chopped
¾ cup flour
1½ teaspoons salt
Pepper to taste

Place vegetables in the oven. Pour juice from clams over vegetables and add enough water to barely cover them. Place on fire and simmer for about 20 minutes or until potatoes are tender. Remove vegetables and juice from oven. DO NOT DRAIN.

Melt butter in oven over medium fire (10-12 briquets) then stir in flour until smooth. Blend in cream until smooth and thick. Add undrained vegetables and clams and heat without boiling. Stir in salt, sugar and pepper. Sprinkle parsley over the top just before serving.

Total cooking time is about one hour.

 "We live on jerky gravy and soggy sourdough bread. Coffee strong as alkali, it's a wonder we ain't dead."

Stella Hughes in *Chuck Wagon Cookin'*

SPRING GARDEN SOUP

When fall brings a little chill to the air and a garden's bounty to the table, try this satisfying soup recipe of Dick and Pat Michaud.

4 medium potatoes, diced
3 medium onions, chopped
4 cups fresh corn, approximately 5-6 ears
¼ lb of salt pork, diced
½ cup water
1 cup carrots
½ cup cut beans
2 teaspoons salt
¼ teaspoon pepper
1 quart milk

Peel and dice potatoes and onions. Using a sharp knife, gently trim kernels of corn from cob. Over low heat, fry pork in an ungreased 12 " Dutch oven for about 3 minutes. Add onion and cook until lightly browned. Combine potatoes, carrots, beans and water and cook over medium heat for about 6 minutes. Add corn and simmer for about 3 minutes. Add salt and pepper and slowly stir in milk. Simmer until hot and carrots are done, then serve with hot rolls. Serves 5-6 people.

CHILE VERDE

Two entrants to the Cookoff—Joseph and Wendy Rodriquez—gave us a good chili recipe.

3 lbs. cubed (1 inch) pork
2 tablespoons whole oregano
1½ teaspoons minced garlic
½ teaspoon cumin seed
2 teaspoons salt
1 teaspoon chili powder (or to taste)
1 can (60-ounce) whole tomatoes, drained
1 can 7-ounce diced green chilies
1 can 7¾-ounce green chili salsa
1 bunch cilantro (or Chinese parsley) chopped
6-8 green onions, chopped

Cook pork in 10 " Dutch oven on high heat, top and bottom, for 2-3 hours. Check periodically, adding hot water as needed if meat becomes too dry. When meat becomes tender, add spices and cook 30 minutes longer. Add remaining ingredients and simmer until meat strings with fork. Serve with flour tortillas, refried beans and Spanish rice.

"Only a damned fool would argue with a skunk, a woman, or a roundup cook."
Stella Hughes in *Chuck Wagon Cookin'*

ENCHILADAS

Here's a favorite south-of-the-border treat. Ole!

Brown and season 1½ lbs. hamburger in your 12" Dutch oven. Drain hamburger and set aside. Wipe out your Dutch oven, heat about ¼-inch oil in the oven and then fry tortillas for a few seconds on each side. Place the tortillas between paper towels to absorb the excess oil. Pour oil out of Dutch oven and wipe the inside again with a paper towel. Cover the bottom of your Dutch oven with tomato sauce. Spoon browned hamburger into the tortillas and roll. Place in Dutch oven with rolled side down. Pour on more tomato sauce and sprinkle grated cheese over the top of the tortillas. Bake with coals on both top and bottom for 10-15 minutes. Cook with coals just on top for another 10-15 minutes. Serve on a bed of lettuce.

RAISIN-FILLED OATMEAL BARS

A recipe for a sweet tooth.

2 cups oatmeal
2 cups flour
1 teaspoon salt
1 teaspoon soda
1 cup brown sugar

1/2 cup shortening
1 egg
1 teaspoon vanilla
1 cup chopped raisins
1/2 cup water
1/2 cup sugar (white)

To make filling, add raisins, water and sugar (white) together and boil. Generously grease a 12" Dutch oven. Mix oatmeal, flour, salt and soda. Add brown sugar, shortening, egg and vanilla. Divide mixture in half. Press one-half of the mixture into greased Dutch oven. Spread raisin filling over oatmeal mixture. Crumble second half of oatmeal mix over filling. Bake from top and bottom for 8-10 minutes over medium coals. Remove Dutch oven from bottom coals and continue baking from top only for an additional 10-12 minutes or until done. May be served from Dutch oven or remove as suggested with pineapple upside-down cake. For variety use raspberry jelly or any of your favorite fillings.

POPCORN

What a neat treat out in the mountains by a campfire.

Over hot coals add 3-5 tablespoons of cooking oil and ⅓-½ cup popcorn to your Dutch oven. Cook, heat and spin the Dutch oven once in a while until popcorn stops popping. Add butter and salt to taste. Enjoy!

"If we were restricted to just one pot or pan for camping or a stay as a castaway on a desert isle, the Dutch oven would be it."
The Fermoyles, Ken and Jean, noted outdoor writers

JB'S FAMOUS "STANDING FORK" CHILI CON CARNE

Mike and Juanita Kohler got to know JB from their mutual interest in Dutch oven cooking. JB lives in California and is an avid year-round Dutch oven cook.

3 lbs USDA choice round steak,	*8-ounce tomato juice*
cut in ¼ inch cubes	*3 Jalapeno peppers,*
1 tablespoon olive oil	*seeded and finely minced*
1 large onion, finely chopped	*10-ounce corn kernels*
3 cloves garlic, finely chopped	*4-ounce chili powder*
1 ¾ cup (14-ounce) clear beef broth	*½ teaspoon cayenne pepper*
1 lb. 14-ounce small red beans	*2 heaping tablespoons*
(about 4 cups)	*corn masa*

Sauté round steak quickly in oil on the bottom of a hot 12" Dutch oven. Add during this process, the onion and garlic. Stir several times until meat is no longer pink. Do not brown meat. Add beef broth (fat-skimmed if necessary). Cook over high heat for 15 minutes.

Add beans, tomato juice, Jalapeno peppers, corn, chili powder and cayenne pepper. Reduce heat to a simmer. Do not boil. Cook for approximately 1 ½ hours. Add corn masa during the last 5 minutes of simmering.

NOTE: This recipe will not be a success if you add to or take from these ingredients. If you use home-made clear beef broth, it must be brought to boil, then refrigerated before fat-skimming.

For your friends South of the border, add 5 Jalapeno peppers and 2 ½ teaspoons of cayenne pepper and ruin the whole thing.

Everyone thinks he makes the best chili in the world. This chili is made on a moderate scale of seasoning to please most anyone. I have had a number of people eat it and report it as "excellent," "very good," etc. Three of another group, each from a different part of Mexico said it was very good but they liked chili which was hotter. They mean "more pepper." It is very simple to make it appealing to the people of Sonora, Jalisco, Mexico City, etc., because the balance that really makes any dish good is present in this recipe; namely the proportion of meat to the amount of the bland ingredients, BEANS. If this proportion is not disturbed, you can add extra seasonings to make it more piquant such as more chiles, more peppers and more salt. You can buy from most stores such products as ground red pepper and "flaked" red pepper. There is also Tabasco brand pepper sauce and another pepper sauce whose brand name is Tapatio (Ta-pah-teeoh), Salsa Picante. This hot sauce and Tapatio must be added with care. (Chili Con Carne seasoning in stores also contains garlic, cumin seed, coriander seeds and oregano.)

The original chili dish was composed first of beans, meat and seasoning. Anything else added to this base makes it "stew." Tomatoes are actually used as a seasoning.

NOTE: Hunt's small red beans in cans can save time of cooking the dry red beans. (Do not use canned chili carne beans as they are already seasoned.) The processed canned beans are low in "gas" and cause less distress in some older people.

JB'S FAMOUS FAR-WEST STEAK AND ROAST BASTE

If you want to add a little savory flavor to your Dutch oven meats, JB recommends using this delectable baste.

1 cup Kikkoman Lite Soy Sauce
2 cups onions, minced
¼ cup Kitchen Bouquet
2 tablespoons garlic, minced

¹/₈ teaspoon Maggi Seasoning
2 tablespoons Beau Monde Seasoning
2 tablespoons honey
2 tablespoons Lea & Perrins Worcestershire Sauce

Combine in blender or food processor. Whirl for one minute. Store in refrigerator. Baste before and during cooking. Imparts better than B-B-Q taste.

Shake well before using.

SWEET 'N EASY BEANS

Gary Bowen and Wally Spring claim that this recipe is good at any picnic or outing and it is also great in a crock pot.

60 oz. pork and beans
½ lb. bacon
1 cup ketchup
1 cup brown sugar

1 cup chopped green peppers
20 oz. crushed pineapple & juice
1 small onion, chopped
1¼ tablespoon liquid smoke

Brown onions, peppers and bacon over hot coals. Add the rest of the ingredients. Place oven over 4-5 coals, with 3-4 coals on top of oven. (Just enough for a real slow simmer.) Grab fishin' pole and come back in 3-4 hours, hungry.

CHAPTER 10

Equipment and Supplies
Satellite Cookoffs/Dutch oven Society
Twin-K Dutch oven accessories
Cookbook order blanks
About the Authors

EQUIPMENT AND SUPPLIES:

The choice of a Dutch oven is critical because it will be both a lifetime investment for you and a family heirloom which you will wish to pass on to your children. The best cast-iron ovens—in the experience of the authors, are those made by the Lodge Mfg. Co. which has been consistently producing quality cast ironware for over three generations. You can find a lot of foreign made ones, primarily from the Far East, but the castings are uneven, the lids generally don't fit well and the authors cannot recommend them.

Most surplus stores, big hardware outlets, sport stores or Boy Scout suppliers stock some Dutch ovens, often in both the castiron and aluminum models. If you can't find any on the shelves, ask the store owner and they can generally order one of the Lodge ovens for you. Garage sales and antique shops will sometimes have an oven, although hardly anyone nowadays wants to let go of their ovens. In buying either a new or used oven, always look it over closely for the quality of the casting, does it have pits in the iron, is it cracked or chipped and does the lid fit and belong to that pot. A faulty pot will never give you satisfaction no matter how good a deal you negotiated.

Dutch oven supplies in the form of tools, tote bags, lid holders, cooking tables, etc. can be obtained from TWIN-K Enterprises. See advertisement in back of the book.

INTERNATIONAL DUTCH OVEN SOCIETY:

If you are a newcomer or an old hand with the black pots you'll enjoy THE association for Dutch Oven Lovers throughout the world. The International Dutch Oven Society (IDOS) is a nonprofit, volunteer-run organization promoting the fun, art and fellowship of Dutch oven cooking. Membership in the IDOS provides each member with the "Dutch Oven News" which is jam-packed with new and delicious recipes; information on cookoff locations and local dutchers; new cooking hints and methods; D.O. classes and equipment and lots of interesting features on the history and people in the Dutch oven world.

And if you are the sort to get really involved, IDOS would be happy to have you join its ranks of volunteers, participants and satellite chairpersons. You can contact the IDOS about membership and activities at the addresses below.

SATELLITE COOKOFFS:

The newest and most exciting activity with the black pots is a Dutch oven cookoff. Youth and/or family member cookoffs make a great event at county fairs, town celebrations, mountainmen rendezvous', festivals, Fourth of July days, family reunions or whatever. Young and old enjoy the fun competition and the chance to learn more about the art of Dutch oven cooking. The smells and sights of a cookoff are natural attractions to the spectators who gravitate to the area and then can't resist leaning over the ropes to find out what's cooking making the cookoff a valuable addition to any civic event.

You can measurably add to your local celebration and probably promote some fellow dutchers by holding a Dutch oven cookoff. IDOS will provide you with all the needed information if you will contact the IDOS at the addresses below.

International Dutch Oven Society
41 East 400 North, #210
Logan, UT 84321

E-mail — *IDOS@idos.com*

Web Page — www.idos.com

"The Dutch Oven Specialists"

DUTCH OVEN ACCESSORIES

For a free brochure and more information write:

TWIN-K™ ENTERPRISES
P.O. Box 4023
Logan, Utah 84323-4023

WORLD CHAMPIONSHIP DUTCH OVEN COOKBOOK

P.O. Box 4024
Logan, Utah 84323-4024

If you would like to order additional copies of the **World Championship Dutch Oven Cookbook,** send $9.95 for each copy plus $4.00 shipping and handling for the first copy and $1.00 shipping and handling for each additional copy. Utah residents include sales tax.

NAME _____

ADDRESS_____

CITY _____ STATE _____ ZIP _____

Make checks payable to World Championship Dutch Oven Cookbook.

WORLD CHAMPIONSHIP DUTCH OVEN COOKBOOK

P.O. Box 4024
Logan, Utah 84323-4024

If you would like to order additional copies of the **World Championship Dutch Oven Cookbook,** send $9.95 for each copy plus $4.00 shipping and handling for the first copy and $1.00 shipping and handling for each additional copy. Utah residents include sales tax.

NAME _____

ADDRESS_____

CITY _____ STATE _____ ZIP _____

Make checks payable to World Championship Dutch Oven Cookbook.

Mike, Juanita, Wallace, Pat

THE KOHLERS

The Kohlers interest in Dutch Oven cooking started many years ago on fishing and scouting adventures in the Rocky Mountains and at family reunions. Mike and his wife Juanita and Wallace and his wife Pat have gained notoriety because of their expertise in Dutch oven cooking. They teach Dutch oven classes for Utah State University and are the co-organizers of the World Championship Dutch Oven Cookoff. Dutch oven catering for businesses, religious, community and civic groups, weddings and reunions is one of their specialities. The Kohlers have been featured in the *Sunset Magazine* and also in newspapers from the *L.A. Times* in California to local newspapers in Utah, Idaho and Wyoming. The Kohlers' love for Dutch oven cooking inspired the founding of their "TWIN-K ENTERPRISES." If you wondered why the name TWIN-K the explanation is easy; Mike and Wallace are TWIN-KOHLER brothers. They design and manufacture Dutch oven accessories which include cooking tables, tools, lid holders and tote bags. Dutch oven cooking for the Kohlers is a family affair starting with building the fire, to preparing, cooking and serving the food and visiting with the guests. They have made some very special friends through their Dutch oven magic.

Pat and Dick

THE MICHAUDS

Dick, like thousands of fellow dutchers, began using the pots as a scoutmaster way back in 1961. He has been called the "Guru" of the Dutch oven by Bob Kellerman of **Lodge Mfg. Co.** He is the founder of the World Championship Dutch Oven Cookoff (WCDOC) as a major event of the Festival of the American West in Logan, UT. Under his chairmanship, the WCDOC brought unparalleled national media coverage to Utah and the Festival including articles in Utah's major papers, the **Los Angeles Times, Western Horseman, Country Home, Sunset Magazine** and their Yearbook, **ABC TV Home Show** and literally dozens of other publications.

He subsequently founded the **International Dutch Oven Society** which grew to over 1000 members and 100 satellite cookoffs throughout the USA while he was the Executive Director. As a result, Dutch oven cooking has experienced a phenomenal resurgence of interest and use throughout North America and has attracted followers even internationally. In truth, many lives have been enhanced because of Dick's efforts on behalf of the Dutch oven movement. Pat is the newcomer to the art of the black pots but she is learning with her usual grace and style. They are grateful for the many friends gained in the process and their cooking with the ovens continues free gratis for their family, friends, church and civic occasions.

NOTES

NOTES